MW00423418

PRAISE FOR *THREE-TIME WORLD CHAMP*

"Thad's story is an American epic from the other side of the page, the innocent to the damned (and back). Sex, drugs, and rock 'n roll."

–Joe Pytka, director and cinematographer

"As the PKA Kickboxing analyst on ESPN—ringside calling Ted Pryor's bouts as he dispatched a long series of opponents—I was naturally very impressed with his kickboxing skills. Add to that my surprise at how interesting and compelling his written words are in his new book *3X World Champ*. It is always intriguing to see the different dimensions of our PKA fighters emerge, but the true life experiences of Ted Pryor are engaging at a whole different level. Whether you like powerful fighters, hard-charging businessmen, and/or people who have come from the 'hard streets' to corporate or financial prominence, you will thoroughly enjoy this unique journey of Ted Pryor—captivating to the very end!"

–Joe Corley, CEO of PKA Worldwide

"This book could be a hit TV series or a blockbuster Hollywood movie! Ted never did anything halfway. It was all or nothing. It's not how many times you get knocked down but how many times you get up! Ted's martial arts background taught him to never give up, and when the going got tough, the tough got going. His life was definitely a roller coaster of highs and lows and highs again. Congratulations on picking yourself up and never giving up until you reached your goals. There are so many life lessons in this book, good and bad. It is truly a story of inspiration and perspiration. So glad it had a happy ending."

–Jeff Smith, 10th Degree Black Belt and first PKA World Kickboxing Champion

"To excel in anything takes dedication and hard work—to become a champion takes even more dedication and hard work. To do it three times is the stuff of legends. That accomplishment alone would make Ted's book a great read. Now, add his complex and fascinating life experience to that and it makes it a must-read! I met Ted Pryor when he produced a film that Eric Roberts and I starred in called *The Butcher*. We became fast friends and spent an engaging fun time together. What I didn't know is what folks will find in his powerful story of crime, business, and danger. Honest and redemptive! Congrats, old friend—a great read! It must be made into a film!"

—Robert Davi, actor, singer, and filmmaker

"The adage 'everyone has a story' certainly applies to Thad (Ted) Pryor. His book *Three-time World Champ* is a compelling story about someone who lived life with its ups and downs. Pryor's ups are sky-high, and his lows are dungeons. This is a story of resilience, grit, and, ultimately, the power of family and the human spirit."

—Maddy Howard, Canadian fitness model and actress

"Prior is the REAL DEAL . . . you might get lucky with one world title, but he's PROVEN—3x world champ!!!! This book's definitely a fun read."

—Bill Gottlieb, producer for Gorilla Pictures

3X
WORLD
CHAMP

3X WORLD CHAMP

The Death-Defying True Story of a
Kickboxer Turned Drug Smuggler . . .
Turned Business Icon

TED PRYOR

BenBella Books, Inc.
Dallas, TX

The events, locations, and conversations in this book, while true, are recreated from the author's memory. However, the essence of the story, and the feelings and emotions evoked, are intended to be accurate representations. In certain instances, names, persons, organizations, and places have been changed to protect an individual's privacy.

Three-Time World Champ copyright © 2024 by Thaddeus Pryor

BenBella Books, Inc.
10440 N. Central Expressway
Suite 800
Dallas, TX 75231
benbellabooks.com
Send feedback to feedback@benbellabooks.com

BenBella is a federally registered trademark.

Printed in the United States of America
10 9 8 7 6 5 4 3 2 1

Library of Congress Control Number: 2024024371
ISBN 9781637745885 (hardcover)
ISBN 9781637745892 (electronic)

Editing by Scott Calamar
Copyediting by James Fraleigh
Proofreading by Becky Maines and Ashley Casteel
Text design and composition by Aaron Edmiston
Cover design by Sarah Avinger
Cover illustration by Sean Hsiao
Printed by Lake Book Manufacturing

For my brother, Tony. My hero.

CONTENTS

AUTHOR'S NOTE

Don't hold me to this. Not everything here is true. But it sure feels like it.

These are the events of my life as I recall them, meaning what you read here may not be exactly how all this shit happened. Time has a way of making the scary things scarier and the good things better, especially when they happened to you. Factor that in. If it's between quotation marks, remember that smugglers don't turn on a tape recorder before a conversation. Finally, know that I've tinkered with some details and left out others to protect those who managed to walk away clean. But even those omissions have most often been accidental because, for all of us, the particulars faded long ago.

All I can say for sure is that I've lived a hell of a life. The story I'll tell you here is the gist of it.

PREFACE

You have to be the toughest son of a bitch in the game. Doesn't matter what game. You gotta be prepared to do anything, maybe everything. Might have to apologize later, might have to pay, but that's the only way you get what you want, what you need in this life. You're either tough or you're on your back.

And I've never been on my back.

PROLOGUE: DECEMBER 1981

"I want this guy right fucking now," said Ray. "He ripped me off for six hundred thousand out of my own safe. Bring him here. Whatever it takes."

"This guy" was Jimmy Savoy, Ray's no-longer-best friend and party pal. A former jockey and racetrack rat from Ray's early days in Florida, Jimmy paid his bills by working as a carpenter with a singular skill: building secret compartments in smugglers' boats so Ray's captains could bring in bales of marijuana undetected by cops and dogs. Now Jimmy had taken on the new role of thief. When the cops busted Ray's smuggling operation out of the Amity Yacht Center in Fort Lauderdale—they'd made me their ticket in, by the way—Jimmy panicked, raided the safe, and hit the highway with the cash, less the expenses of a new car and an old hooker.

This explained his latest role: fugitive from Ray's Miami Marijuana Mafia.

The crew would find him for sure. The only question was how much torture they would inflict before relieving the man's suffering with a bullet in the head.

As for me, I guess I wanted to hear the reality out loud, needed to erase any kidding myself about exactly where I was. So I spoke, and this is what naïve sounds like: "Ray," I said, "what are you gonna do when you get him?"

"You know exactly what I'm gonna do," he said. Little Ray Thompson, the king of cannabis, grinned at me from under his stringy, '70s-Florida-summer head of hair.

"Unless, you hero kickboxing fuck, you wanna do it for me."

And there it was. "Whaddya say to a little wet work, champ? Wanna pop your cherry?"

Chapter 1

FIGHTER

When I was a kid, I never planned on being a fighter. But sometimes a plan's got nothing to do with where you end up.

I grew up in Queens, New York. If you've never seen photos of Queens in the early 1960s, think of a gangster movie minus the gangsters: concrete stoops and cracked sidewalks in front of working-class homes next to the middle-class homes next to the bodega and the market and the butcher and the barber and the candy store. We were at 216-45 114th Avenue off of Springfield Boulevard.

My family was modern and middle class. My father, Hugh Francis. My mother, Concetta Caruso. Three older sisters, Henrietta, Mary, Consuela, and a brother, Anthony. I was the youngest, Thaddeus John Xavier Aloysius. Big name for a scrawny kid. Might as well paint a target on my forehead.

I went to Sacred Heart Catholic School, but I wasn't much of a student. One time my mom asked me about my grades, and I told her they were fantastic. She said, "That's not what the F stands for."

I repeated the first grade twice. The only reason they moved me up sounds like a punchline: I outgrew the desk. I wasn't lazy. I had dyslexia and attention-deficit disorder back before those things had names. That's why I got interested in athletics and martial arts and taking care of my body, but we're not to that part yet.

By 1968, my mom's arthritis was so bad that we moved to Florida. Dad thought the warmer weather might help. We settled in a little town called Miramar. You haven't heard of it. Nobody has. We were twenty miles from Miami. That'll be big later, too.

Even with the arthritis, Mom took a job waiting tables. Dad was a ticket agent for Greyhound, but we still didn't have enough money, so he took a second job with Gray Line Tours plus whatever else extra he could find. This kept him out of the house 7 AM to midnight, so I didn't see much of him. We declined in financial status, but now we had a swimming pool. Florida. Go figure.

My friends and I played lots of games, real ones plus the ones we made up, and plenty from the borough: stickball, wiffle ball, dodgeball, Chinese handball, stoopball. In Queens I was only an average athlete, but here, for some reason, I was jock of the block. If there was a ball, I was in, and my team would win.

Then there were the fights. Nothing organized, just the bullshit kids get into. I was ten years old but a couple grades behind my age, so that gave me an advantage—not that I used it in this case. I was happy to start fights because I didn't have to finish them. I might throw a rock, hit some bigger kid in the back of the head. I'd run home, the kid a few steps behind. When we got to the front porch, I'd duck inside while my brother Anthony would come out and beat his ass.

Then my shit came back around. There was this kid named Rodney Barnes. He was weird, a ten-year-old going on twenty, and he looked like a half-sized frat boy. The other kids figured I was the guy to put him away. Didn't they know I farmed this stuff out to my brother? The kids got Rodney to start something with me and, in a few days, mission accomplished: one afternoon on the playground, we duked it out. I got lucky and won.

That wasn't a good outcome. If this monster-looking kid hadn't folded like a paper sack, I'd have been fine—embarrassed, but that'd be all right because nobody remembers the loser in a schoolyard fight. Instead, the skinny, scrawny kid from New York knocked over the giant. That made me the toughest guy in the school by reputation, if not ability. It also made me the target of every kid in the fifth grade who wanted the title. I'd had one real fight in my life, and I'd won it not because I was any good but because Rodney was even worse. Or maybe he threw it. It didn't matter now. It wasn't more than a couple days before someone took their shot. He was a lot younger and a lot tougher, and he kicked my ass.

I should have let it go but I didn't. The next day I went after him with the old plan: I'd hit him with a rock and run like hell to Anthony. Except when I got to the front porch, it wasn't Anthony waiting. "You need to learn," said my father, and shut the door. The kid wailed on me until he got bored with it. Then it was Dad's turn.

"Number one," he said, "your brother's not always going to be there to fight your battles. Neither am I. Number two, if you make your bed, you gotta lie in it." Then he said something else. "I'm going to pay for you to have karate lessons."

Chapter 2

KARATE KID

The next day we were up the street at Olympic Karate, a dojo on Pembroke Road. Dad presented me to the sensei, a guy named Jim Martin. "I'll pay for the first month," my father told me. "After that, it's up to you."

Karate became everything to me, and instantly. I was lousy at school, I had farmed out my fights to my brother, but this was different. I felt confidence. I felt security. I was good at this, I got good fast, and it was all mine. Mr. Martin liked me so much that he gave me a job, made me the karate kid before there was a *Karate Kid*. Whatever he needed doing, I did. Sweep. Vacuum. Clean toilets. Didn't matter to me. I was trading my work for karate lessons.

Mr. Martin was of course free to decide that I had come up short. To avoid that problem, I started mowing lawns. Eventually I had twenty accounts, which at age thirteen I sold to a landscaping company for $1,500—a budding businessman, but that's one more thing we'll get to later. I got a job at a gas station, too. Joe Ripple ran the place. He walked around 24/7 doing an impression of Billy Jack, the kickass hippie from the movie of the same name. Billy Jack was a native American, a Vietnam vet, and a hapkido master whose philosophy of life can be summarized as "peace through pain." I don't know how much, besides being a vet, that short, squat Joe really had in common with lean and mean Billy Jack, but Joe Ripple loved karate the same way I did, and he kept me around less to work than to pick up whatever I was learning at the dojo.

By age seventeen I had earned a black belt in kumite, a sparring style of Korean karate. I learned it as a no-contact discipline, with an emphasis on absolute control. You'd throw a kick to a guy's face, but you'd have to be able to pull it back, stop within an inch of him. Close is good, closer is better, but contact is a no-go. Same with throwing a full punch. You wanna put so much behind it that if it connects, it'll crush a guy's nose, but in kumite you have to be able to stop before the target. This would be valuable later because it gave my punches spectacular precision.

In those few years I quickly collected a range of skills and techniques well beyond my age. I went to every karate competition I could find and won most of them. Lots of trophies, lots of medals. I liked the recognition. More than that, I liked winning. More than either, though, I loved the pursuit of martial arts, the mastery I was gaining, the self-discipline, and the meaning it was giving to my life.

This wasn't the kind of success anybody would have predicted for me. Nobody in our family was any kind of model of health and fitness. Except for one sister and me, everybody smoked. As for fighting prowess, my brother was the only one who had that, and at this point

I should admit that the kids I led to the front porch weren't the only ones he beat up. Tony liked to fight because he was good at it, and at least once a week he'd kick my ass just to stay in practice. Me being a martial artist wouldn't have crossed anybody's mind. And a world champion? *Fuhgeddaboudit!* You might as well have told people that Ted was gonna be the king of England.

While I was discovering this new path for myself, Tony had done a hitch in the Navy. On his return, our mom gave him a warning: "Your little brother may not be a pushover anymore." Tony didn't believe her.

He'd left behind a closet full of sharp clothes. In his absence I had regularly availed myself of the bounty of his good taste. I'd head out at night in one of his best shirts and jackets, plus a pair of his coolest shoes. The first night he was back he stopped me as I was leaving. "Take off the shirt, kid," he said.

"Bro, I'm wearing this and you'd better not try to stop me. I don't want to hurt you, especially on your first day back. The Navy doesn't need a sailor with a broken arm, do they?"

It was beyond him to believe I'd gotten tough. Even if he thought I was up to a fight, Tony didn't believe I'd follow through, surely not with him, whose fight record with me was all wins, no losses. "I know all about your kung fu crap," he said. "You might flip your little karate friends on a mat, but I'm not scared of you."

He put himself between me and the door. Keep in mind that this wasn't over a disagreement on any matter of any kind. This was whether I could wear a two-year-old polyester disco shirt. We both understood this was less a matter of principle and more a ceremonial "welcome home" ass-whooping to remind me that he still ruled the roost. "You can take that karate stuff and pound it up your ass."

"That what you think?"

"You come past me, Thad, I'll knock your block off."

I let him take the first swing because I wouldn't need one. I ducked. He missed. That made him mad, and he took a step closer, exactly where I wanted him. In one motion I had him in a choke-hold, a move as easy for me as breathing. As the resistance dribbled out of him, I eased my brother to the floor. He went limp, then he passed out cold.

Half a minute later my mother was hitting me over the head with a broom. "Stop it! You're killing him!"

"He'll live," I said. "He's just gonna sleep for a while." I laid him flat next to the couch, straightened my shirt—*his shirt*—stepped over him, and walked out the door.

When I came home, Tony was waiting for me. No surprise. We were brothers. But now I'd find out that this had been more than just another fight.

"Hey, Thad. You wanna wear my stuff, that's fine."

"Y'okay?"

He nodded, yeah. "So . . . how the hell d'you do that?"

"I can't just show you. It's training. Gotta spend some serious time with it. That's what I've been doing. I wasn't too tough before . . ."

"You got it now, bro," he said. "I thought that martial arts stuff was baloney. Guess not. Turns out you're a badass."

Turns out you're a badass. There's nothing Tony could have said that would have made me prouder. My brother, the one who had always protected me when I was in a jam? He had just told me to my face that I was a tough guy now, just like him. He'd even said it with pride.

Brothers always love each other because they're family, but respect has to be earned. I'd always wanted Tony's respect. Now I had it. I'd always be his little brother, but now, in this way, we'd be on the same level. I liked that a lot.

There it was, happening again: the past being a shitty predictor of how things turn out. I'd experience that truth over and over.

I stayed with Mr. Martin until he moved away. His departure meant I needed a new sensei. I was a black belt, but I knew that no matter how good you are, or how good you think you are, every student of karate needs a sensei.

That's when I met Big Joe Hess. He was six feet two, 230 pounds, and a powerhouse. He was opening a dojo on Sunrise Boulevard. Across town at Olympic, I was, by age seventeen, teaching thirty students of all levels—white belts, yellow belts, green belts, brown belts, a couple black belts. Most of them followed me to Joe's place. Since my green belts were beating his black belts, Joe had me teach all the classes at his dojo. More important to me, though, was that Joe could teach me. Even with the difference in age and experience, we made a helluva pair. My kicks were already so fast that the only way Joe could get the advantage on me was to rely on his size. He'd rush me at the top and sweep me—that is, he'd do a jujitsu move to hit my ankle and bring me to the floor. I had great technique, though. Better than Joe's, and he was already a legend.

Before he made karate his main thing, Joe had been a cop in New Jersey. He still kept a hand in, training officers at the Broward County Police Academy in self-defense and riot control. He was so good that in a few years he would do his stuff as a stunt man in pictures like *Bad Boys II* and *Ace Ventura*, other times as a tough-guy actor in the *Nash*

Bridges and *Miami Vice* TV series. He was even in *The Bodyguard* with Kevin Costner and Whitney Houston.

Our connection grew quickly and it grew deep. When my mother died around age fifty of cancer—too damn young—Joe and his wife, Brenda, treated me like their own son, and not just while I grieved. They made me a member of their family.

Chapter 3

TED

Joe found an extra job for me, something that would put some cash in my pocket while putting my skills to use: security guard at a psychiatric hospital. They needed someone who could literally kick ass—and leg, and back. If a patient went at somebody, I was there to bring the pain. Most of the patients weren't a threat to anybody, but the ones who really were could do it without breaking a sweat. Also, this was an all-male facility, so there was constant competition to be the biggest swinging dick on the block, and the competition was fierce. The only way to stop one of those guys was to get on top of him right away, otherwise it was like trying to stop a train. If one of those fights got going, all you could do was wait for it to be over, then hose the mess off the concrete and put on your suit jacket so you'd look decent at the funeral.

I hear you're not supposed to say "criminally insane" anymore, but what else could you say about a lot of these guys? They were criminals by conviction and insane by behavior. You come up with a better word, I'm all ears.

From the perspective of a guy whose job was to keep them from getting too physical, there were only three kinds of patients. First were those who took psychiatric medication every day, which somehow made them stronger. Second were those who occasionally missed their psychiatric medication, which somehow made them stronger. Third were those popping steroids like Tic Tacs, which somehow made them stronger. To put a bow on all that, a few of these monsters had a second address on death row. That made my little acre of hell their own personal vacation home—you know, where they could let their hair down a little bit and beat people up for sport. It's not like they had anything else to do, right? Plus, what could the punishment be? If you're already in a hospital for the criminally insane, there's not some worse place to go.

I'm making a joke. It's impossible to work in a place like that and not gain a new understanding of how hard life can be. Some of these guys had suffered their whole lives. Maybe it was in their genes, maybe they'd been made this way by parents or circumstances. Probably a little of both. Some choose to be evil, sure, but some lived a life from early on that made that bad choice a lot easier. I'm not excusing it. I'm saying for some people, violence just makes sense. Hence the need for guys like me to stand in the gap. If you've spent your life pissed or crazy or both and you work out all day, every day, once in a while you're gonna hurt somebody just to be sure your engine's running.

I never understood why anybody thought the smart play was to give stone-cold killers benches, barbells, and bumper plates. Giving violent prisoners weightlifting equipment is like giving Jack the Ripper the keys to the knife counter at a sporting goods store. I'd want 'em all slim and weak—though if you took away the workout stuff, they'd probably just tear the stools out of the concrete and bash each other anyway.

The typical altercation went like this: a six-foot-four, 300-pound guy, about three doses ahead or behind on some psychoactive medicine, stomps into the day room and threatens to toss nurses like darts in a sports bar or slam doctors against the wall like they were hanging those white coats on pegs.

I'd grab two or three other guards and we'd go in with these instructions: chase him down, then talk him down. I was to subdue a guy with force only if necessary, preferably without hurting him. That was the hard part. I could shut it down by breaking his arm or cracking his skull, easy, but that wasn't allowed except as a last resort. That meant our primary weapon was intimidation. My presence alone was supposed to be enough to get someone to do a little mental calculation: I can back down now, or get my ass kicked and back down later. Guys like me needed to be able to do more than just inflict pain. But we had to be just as good at making people think that if they got out of line, pain was on the way. The key to making that threat work is breathing, focus, steadiness, and concentration. My martial arts training served me well.

Sometimes I had to get physical anyway, and I had a method that maximized effect and minimized the blood. My go-to move was to hit the guy in the celiac plexus, that spot where your rib cage splits, the center of a network of nerves that send a pain signal everywhere in the body. Taking a hit there is like dropping a hand grenade on a gas pump: the effects blow in every direction.

Not that there wasn't a menu of painful goodness I could choose from otherwise. I could whip up a few other treats like punching the Adam's apple or applying a chokehold. Once you have a guy gasping for air, you have his undivided attention. I did that many times, and with more than a little pride—not for hurting the guy but for turning down the heat in a situation that was dangerous for everyone, and doing so efficiently. It's a powerful feeling, that ability to channel physical strength into responsible domination. There's not much more satisfying than approaching an attacker and a scrum of his potential victims and de-escalating things immediately.

When I was in grade school, I only pretended I was cock of the walk—my brother had to back up my boasting. Now I was in a truly dangerous place on a daily basis, and I didn't need anybody to back me up. I liked the feeling. I was doing something that mattered. I was pretty damn good at it, too, and everybody knew it. That's probably why Joe got me a new job, helping him in his police training classes. I liked dealing with law enforcement officers. That would change a few years later—one more thing we'll get to soon.

Joe did something else to help me, simple for him but the most important thing for me. Around this time, full-contact martial arts were becoming popular. With this opportunity all over the sports page and even the front page, I decided that I had to turn pro. It was what I wanted more than anything. The only question was how to do it. Fortunately, Joe came through one more time. He was already a pro and an aspiring world champion. A few phone calls from him to the right guys, that's all it took.

My first professional fight was set, the first of what would go on to be a run of seventy through 1987. I also realized that I wanted more than just to be in the game. I would do whatever it took to become not only a good kickboxer or a great kickboxer. I set out to be the champion of the world. Everything else would be secondary.

Look up my records and you'll find they're all credited to "Ted" Pryor. Except Ted isn't the name I was born with, as I mentioned. My dad wanted me to have a very dignified name, something dramatic and memorable, so he chose "Thaddeus." During my youth that's what people called me, sometimes shortened to "Thad." He may have been proud of the name, but at school it made me want to hide under my desk. You know how kids are. I thought it was quirky at best and humiliating at worst. But the only thing worse than that feeling would be disappointing Dad by telling him I didn't like the name.

It was the night of that first professional fight: a three-rounder, part of a night of fights at the Nassau Coliseum just outside New York City. It was what every ambitious fighter dreams about, a debut in one of the most famous fight venues in the world, and under the mentorship of one of the greats. To top it off, the referee was Chuck Norris. He was already famous and, when we met, he turned out to be as awesome as I had hoped. We'd end up friends for life. And my opponent wasn't just some jamoke. I was going up against Teddy Wong, the famous student of the even more famous Bruce Lee.

The bell sounded, the fight started, and my mind was one hundred percent in the ring. Yet something was creeping into my concentration. It sounded great. It pushed me forward, even gave me energy: "Go, Thad! Go, Thad! Go, Thad!" The crowd was cheering for me!

In the quick minute between rounds, I bragged to Joe, who was working as my corner man. "You hear that?" I said.

"I sure do!" he said, and he laughed.

"What are you laughing about? They're shouting my name."

"No, they're not. They're saying, '*Go, fag!*'"

In those days it was a slur people got away with, from schoolyards to boardrooms and even on TV. Doesn't make it right, and I'm not defending it, I'm just telling you what happened the first time I was in the ring.

"'Go, fag'? Ya sure?" I said.

"Yeah, I'm sure," said Joe. "Can't you hear it?"

I still didn't get it. "Who's the fag?" I said.

"You are!" he said. "They can't say *Thad!*"

The bell rang and I was back in the ring, distracted but still doing my job. The chanting kept on. They shouted it between rounds. They shouted it when I was up. They shouted it when I was down. Thanks to that, this was my first and last fight under my given name. From then on, I would be Ted, which is a lot easier to shout.

Not long after, I explained to my father what I'd done with my professional name and why I'd done it. He was disappointed, as I knew he would be, but he understood. With that unpleasantness behind me, I took on my official identity as a fighter, the one you'll find in the record books today: Ted Pryor, on his way, I hoped, to becoming world champion.

Chapter 4

FREELANCER

I f you're a pro player in football or baseball, you're sitting pretty when it comes to cash, at least in the years you're playing. Any other sport, you have to do something else to pay the bills. I was a kickboxer, which doesn't put food on your table or gas in your car, so I looked for even more jobs. Joe, bless him, got me moved up at the academy. Now I'd be a correctional counselor, what they called a CC-One, at the Pompano Correctional Office, a work-release facility, working with guys headed out of state prison and back into the world. I was one of the youngest counselors in Florida. Instead of $50 a week, they were going to pay me $600 a month, excellent money for the time and crazy money at my age. I quit the institution. No more of the criminally insane proving it by trying to knock the teeth out of my head. I'd still be dealing with muscled-up tough guys—I seem to attract the type—but these wouldn't be looking for trouble. They'd be trying to stay out of it. And if a fight broke out anyway, I could skip over the calm-down talk and just hit 'em.

I had to submit nightly reports, except I couldn't read very well and I couldn't spell at all. My boss liked my work enough that he thought it was worth doing the writing for me. I'd tell him what went on and he'd scribble it down. For this concession he got a reliable employee who did the work well.

A guy named Barry Eringer started at the same time. Barry was bright and had a college degree. Having the second doesn't guarantee the first, but Barry had both. We spent a lot of time together. He would be my best man at my first wedding. We were about the same age, and he was great to work with. A few years later, we would reconnect in this same place, but in a very different way.

The job was a welcome step up from the psychiatric hospital. The place was an open space without bars on the windows, but still with head counts like before, plus a schedule that told everyone where to be and when to be there. I was still a guard, but instead of a unform, I wore a jacket and a tie. My responsibilities were to ensure that the men were either productively occupied, in bed asleep, or offsite at their jobs. I worked an eight-hour shift with a start time that moved ahead each month: thirty days starting the day at 8 AM, the next thirty days at 3 PM, the next at 11 at night, then back to the morning.

The thing about being a guard is that they have to respect you, even fear you a bit. But everything goes smoother if they like you a little, too. I got popular with the inmates because most of them were young and I was, too. We had something else in common: we shared a respect for people with athletic skill and discipline. It helped that they knew I was a fighter, which they thought was pretty good. So did I.

Work paid the bills, but the real pleasure came from elsewhere.

Joe was in line for a shot at the title. Of course, I wanted to be a world champion, too, so he made a generous offer. "Why don't you train with me?" He didn't have to ask twice. We sparred every day. Sometimes we'd go down to Angelo Dundee's Fifth Street Gym and work on our boxing. Great days.

My discipline and natural skill had a lot to do with my success as a fighter. I learned a lot, first from Mr. Martin and then, of course, from Joe. But I also have to credit Angelo and the guys at the gym, because it was there that I learned from the best of their generation, maybe the best of all time. There was Sugar Ray Leonard—"sweet as sugar," that's how he got his name. Dazzling combinations and dancer's footwork. Then there was Roberto Durán, who came to America from Panama and earned the nickname "*Manos de Piedra*," meaning "Hands of Stone." I learned firsthand that was true, or maybe I should say I learned first-fist; the man could punch like a rock. Roberto fought across five decades and into the twenty-first century, the first fighter since the Galveston Giant, Jack Johnson, to stay in the ring so many years. I still remember how it felt to get hit by him. Wow. Then there were my own colleagues, my guys, names known by every fan. I could fill this book with stories about all those men, but I'll tell you about only two of them.

Steve Shepherd is a five-time world champion kickboxer—he even managed to take me in a split decision. (Neither of us could get the KO, so it went to the cards.) Steve was the first big promoter of kickboxing events. He proved that the sport could be financially viable. In other words, without Steve, we wouldn't have turned our talents into paydays.

Don "The Dragon" Wilson is an eleven-time world champion with forty-seven KOs, and he's one of the greatest martial artists of all time. Don always said he was a kicker, that was his thing, and not so much a puncher. Still, he was good with either the right or the left, one more thing that made him a killer in the ring. Like most of us, he ended up doing what we do in front of the movie cameras. You probably saw him in *Batman Forever*, for instance, or, in the 2000s, in *The Last Sentinel* and *Soft Target*, a couple of pictures I produced.

Less than a year after Joe and I began training together, he would win the fight he'd trained for, the one we'd worked toward side by side. Now he was the world heavyweight champion for the Professional Karate Association, one of the two main professional kickboxing organizations in the US and Europe. He knocked out Ernie Hyman—no slouch, that guy—in a three-round bout in front of nearly four thousand fans at the Nassau Coliseum, where he'd given me my professional start.

Now Joe was a champion of the world. I was working hard to join him.

When you're a martial artist whom people have heard of, you get offers to be a bodyguard. Ed Parker was a great martial artist, the founder of American Kenpo Karate. One day he was giving a demonstration in Beverly Hills when Elvis Presley came in, then sat down to watch. Elvis had already studied karate while in the service and was fascinated by it. He and Ed became lifelong friends, and Ed taught him for many years. When Elvis set out on what would be his last tour, he decided that his bodyguards had to be martial artists, all accomplished black belts. Ed knew Joe Hess, and that's how Joe and I ended up as Elvis's bodyguards for his last shows.

By this time, Elvis was a bitter man. He was always nice to Joe and me—he gave me one of his blue scarves, and it's framed on my wall—but he was angry and unhappy and it showed. In his mind, all the fame didn't begin to balance the scales against the loss of his mother, his wife, and most of his fortune. The emotional pain was matched by his prison of a body. He was north of 350 pounds, very uncomfortable, and sweating whenever he moved, so much that he hated to be touched. For about a dozen concerts over the course of more than a year, Joe and I were the two guards next to Elvis himself, the last line of defense against fans, especially women, trying to break through the barricade of protectors around him after a show. A few managed to reach me before they got to the King. I went undefeated in fending them off, usually with a chokehold around the body instead of the neck. I'd ease them to the floor, then the nearest guy on our team would take them back where they came from. The gig came to an end not with a big, end-of-tour party but a short phone call in the afternoon. Elvis was dead at only forty-two. Tragic.

My other memorable bodyguard job was years later for *Miami Vice* actor Don Johnson. His wife, Melanie Griffith, was a sweetheart, and even more gorgeous in person than in the movies. Don didn't know me personally, but he knew who I was, so when he needed someone to look out for him, he sought me out. I didn't want the job but it sounded interesting, so I decided to give it a month. I lasted ten days.

Don was moody, and that's putting it nicely. One day he told me to pick up his dry cleaning.

"Excuse me?"

"You heard me, boy. Go pick up my dry cleaning."

"I'm your bodyguard, not your boy," I said. "Nobody speaks to me like that, including you."

"I'll speak to you however I want," he said.

I didn't want the job much anyway, and it didn't matter to me what the pay or the prestige was if the price would be saying "Yes, sir" to disrespect. "Tell you what," I said. "We're done here. I won't leave you unprotected, so I'm going to call a replacement, then I'm going outside and wait for him."

"You're nothing but a punk," he said.

"You're lucky I have thick skin," I said. "Otherwise I'd bitch-slap you right here in front of your wife." He didn't have much to say to that, so he stormed off. I let him. I called my replacement, then hugged Melanie and told her goodbye as she apologized for her husband's dick move. A few years later, thank goodness, she'd figure out that she, like me, deserved better.

Chapter 5

LUCKY MAN

When it comes to love, I did a hell of a lot better than Melanie did. Early on I was blessed to meet the first great love of my life. I was seventeen, full of ambition, and things were going my way in the ring and with my job. Success in those things, and at a young age, makes a young man confident with girls, too. I believed I could charm any woman I wanted. On this day I put it to the test.

The competition to be the hottest girl on Hollywood Beach is steep any day of the week, but on this day there was no contest. Enter Tonita Queen, as beautiful a girl as I'd ever seen because she was as beautiful a girl as has ever been: dark hair, tanned skin, the smile, the figure, the glow. Even in a crowd of other beach beauties she stood out. That I met her on a perfect day under a perfect sky on a perfect Florida beach only added to the mystique.

A buddy and I were throwing a flying disc when I saw her, and it struck me like a bolt of lightning. I didn't have to think about it. I didn't want to point her out to my buddy or just stand there and admire her. I felt more than an attraction; I felt a connection, and I knew this was something more than I'd felt before.

Unfortunately, the seriousness of my feelings didn't suddenly equip me with any more sophisticated tools in my arsenal to meet her than any other high school boy would have had. I did the only thing I knew to do—make my pitch—except I did it right away, no waiting. I asked my buddy to fluff a throw so it would land near her. I raced in her direction, made a leap to catch the disc, and missed. I came down next to her, kicking up a spray of sand all over her legs—her perfect legs, I have to add. Not the glorious catch I had in mind, but it got me next to her.

I gave her my game anyway: the apology for the sand, to start, plus now I had an excuse to try to brush it off of her. The usual small talk followed, which is the same whether you're on a beach or in a bar, except I was more nervous than I would have been. I guess that meant I really did know at some deep level that this mattered. The fact that she didn't ignore me was all the encouragement I needed to finally go for more than chatter and introduce myself.

"I know who you are," she said.

"Really? How?"

"I've seen you around. You're the martial arts guy." She knew me! I was in heaven, and she was an angel.

Does a girl know how nervous a guy gets when he's trying to impress her? Or is she just as nervous as the guy? I didn't know then, and I don't know today. All I knew for certain was this was going my way, she wasn't trying to shoot me down, and, if her vibes were any indication, she felt the same connection I was feeling.

I opened my mouth to say whatever would come out next when this happened: a seagull flew close to my face and took a drippy shit right on my lip. Did she see it? I didn't wait around to find out. I turned and ran for the water. "Hey, Tonita! I'm gonna get in for a while!" Never mind that we were in the middle of a conversation, I couldn't let her see me with bird shit on my face. I cleaned up in the surf, tried to look like I was out there having fun, and came right back. If she saw the bird mess, she didn't say anything to me about it.

They say if you get pooped on by a bird, it's good luck. I don't know about that. All I know is, that afternoon on the beach was the beginning of one of the most wonderful relationships in my life. Tonita and I were immediately inseparable. I felt like the luckiest guy ever. I didn't yet know what would turn out to be true: that this wonderful woman and I would be wrapped up together—for good times and wild times and hard times—for the rest of our lives.

I used my first paycheck from the work-release center to take Tonita on our first date, just one of many good things that came from my time working there. It was a place where people showed me respect and where I felt great satisfaction for a job well done. In addition, the arrangement helped me keep pushing ahead in the martial arts. I was prepping for real matches and a shot at the title. The loose supervision presented an opportunity.

A couple times a week, I would take some of the inmates to the park and spar with them. I'd throw some gloves and helmets in the van and off we'd go—not exactly standard procedure, but we got away with it. Things were relaxed here, the people I worked for liked me, and the prisoners weren't gonna snitch me out for giving them an afternoon away. They'd pair off against each other, and just as often I'd get in the ring with them for a two- or three-round match. They were glad to be out of the building, and there isn't a prisoner alive who wouldn't want to take a swing at a guard—but, as I said, they didn't see me as the enemy. They were on the way out, and they thought of me as someone who was helping them. We did fight for sport, though, and I'd usually put them on their backs, but they didn't mind. When you're out from under regular supervision, you'll put up with a lot. Plus they liked finding out that someone in my position would let 'em take an honest swing back. And they especially liked the fact that they were fighting a pro, though they usually learned my status the hard way. More than once I heard someone say, "*Day-um,* this white boy can fight!"

Still, my pro career wasn't going the way I had planned. I have a pretty high opinion of myself, but when you're in the ring, it's not your opinions that count. What matters is what you can inflict on your opponent, and what you can take and still be standing. I had taken my first four professional fights in quick succession. I'd lost them all. At the end of that fifth fight, when the decision came down against me one more time, I had to reassess the way I'd been pursuing my dream. A dreamer trying to make it in the real world has to face the situation with eyes wide open. I wasn't losing because I lacked the skills. I was losing because I was full of myself. I had mistaken confidence for preparation. I hadn't been winning because I hadn't been putting in the sweat and the hard work it takes to be a champ. I had the talent. I just hadn't been cultivating it.

I was a great athlete, but the kind of skill it takes to be a champ is like a blade: if you don't keep it sharp, it won't cut a thing. Somehow I'd gotten it in my head that my skills were permanent, always on call, a thing that was just a part of me that I didn't have to take care of. I was wrong. A champ busts his ass in that gym day in, day out. If you're not always getting stronger, you're always getting weaker. Now that I saw the truth, I had to train. I needed stamina. I needed legs that would never give out. I needed to be able to take a punch like a man takes a breath, my body so inured to the feeling that it hardly even registered.

At that point, I was no champ. I was hard as stone for a round, maybe two, but past that I'd get tired, stop scoring points. Yeah, I'd never been knocked down, but with the attitude I'd been bringing to the ring, it wouldn't be long before that run got broken. So, as I stood in the dressing room, amid the stink of having lost all five of the only professional fights to my name, I declared the end of one thing and the start of another. I said this to myself, said it like an oath: *I'm not gonna lose again.*

Before I retired in 1987, I'd fight another sixty-five fights. I'd win every one of them.

It was like turning on a light. I was lost, and then I was found. I changed my attitude. My body would follow. I made sure of it. I wasn't a champion yet—just a guy with a lot of promise—but now I would set myself on a course that would work. It would demand more of me, and that was fine. Whatever it takes.

The next day, I matched my transformed outlook with a brand-new routine. Now I was doing karate every day with new commitment, sparring with the greats and soon-to-be-greats. Within weeks I was taking ranked matches and winning them. The fights were getting more and more intense, and that was good. I dedicated myself to training. A spare minute of the day was a minute I'd use to feed my mind and condition my body. It was a good life and a demanding life, but I was holding up my end of the deal with the universe for the payoff I'd promised myself lay ahead.

I had decided to make going after my championship dreams my first priority. Joe had opened that door. Now I would meet a man who would open a door to something even more influential.

Chapter 6

FIRST-TIMER

"How'd you like to make five grand?"

It was an offer from my sister's new husband. I knew him a little. His name was Steve Chiappa. "Whaddya say, Ted?"

He asked twice because I was too stunned to answer the first time. "For that kind of money, Steve? I'll do anything."

He pointed to a car. "I need you to drive that from here to Fort Myers." It was an easy trip, east to west across Florida, a couple hours on an interstate highway known as Alligator Alley. I wouldn't even have to put the miles on my own car.

"That's all I gotta do?"

"That's all you gotta do," he said. "Bring your girlfriend if you want. In fact, you probably should." He paused. "Looks better that way."

It was South Florida in 1978. Down here nobody with a pulse didn't know what this was. I figured he had a few bundles of marijuana in that car, maybe a couple hundred pounds, bound for some dealer on the Gulf Coast. A little back-of-the-envelope arithmetic will tell you that with street prices at the time of about $12 an ounce, that delivery was worth between $40,000 and $50,000—more if you cut the stuff for the street. The five grand he promised me would be about 10 percent of his take. Anybody in any commercial operation, legit or otherwise, will tell you that's a reasonable cost of doing business. No way around the expense. He was doing me a solid, giving me the opportunity instead of somebody else.

Fifty grand's a lot even now, but back then it really was in *wow* territory. The average family income in the US was a little over $22,000. I was making less than a third of that. The five Gs tossed my way was most of a year's income, a fortune. Steve, or whoever was behind him, was swinging in the big leagues. I told him yes. What else was I gonna say?

One more time, this wasn't the outcome anyone would have expected from me. When I was still at home, I wasn't just a good kid, I was a straight arrow. To tell the truth, I was a narc. My brother learned that firsthand. One day when I was twelve, I was rummaging through his things—he was going to beat me up anyway, so I might as well give him a reason, right?—and I came across a bag of pot. I was scandalized and I flushed it. When he figured out it was gone, he set the world record for being pissed. When he figured out I was the one who took it, he broke that record. And when I told him I'd flushed it, he took the gold medal in beating the snot out of a little brother.

Where'd that kid go? It's not a hard question. It's not like I'd been a straight arrow because of some deeply held principles. The chance came to make some money if I stopped being a straight arrow, so I did. At that age, and in the weed-drenched world of South Florida, I didn't see any good reason to turn down money for making a pot run that would put most of a year's income in my pocket. Just because pot wasn't for me didn't mean it wasn't for other people. I knew that firsthand.

A little before this, when I was working as a CC-One in the work-release facility, my mother was dying of pancreatic cancer. The treatment of choice was chemotherapy. It was the only thing that might have saved mom from the hell of cancer, or at least added some time to her life. The problem is that chemo comes with a hell of its own. The treatments left her in agonizing pain. After a day's round of the drugs, she'd throw up all night. There weren't any medicines in the hospital to give her any relief, but there was something else that could. Everybody knew this, but not everybody was willing to do something about it.

With my mother in agony, I got her marijuana. I got it from my brother. It brought her relief in a situation where nothing legal could help. It made her better in every way, with the vomiting, with the pain, with the inability to sleep amid the wracking ache from the disease, the treatment, and the battle they were fighting against each other inside her body. I like to think the hospital staff knew what I was doing and that they looked the other way. Doctors and nurses see enough pain. Surely they would be grateful for anything that helped so much while hurting no one. This was my introduction to pot as something other than a dangerous, evil thing. Because of this illegal drug, my mom could get through her final hours without gritting her teeth and crying out for hours in pain.

I was a teenager. Life was confusing enough, but this choice was clear. The laws are gonna say what they say. Doing the right thing is often a different question. Did this experience make it easier for me to justify what came later? Of course it did, but that's beside the point. As I watched my mother die, I chose to do something without a thought to any consequences except her relief.

And then my mother died. She passed in a lot less pain than the law would have forced on her. I didn't care then if what I did was legal. I still don't. I did what was right. I don't regret a thing.

I learned that breaking a rule the first time makes it easier to break it next time. How long and how far will somebody color outside the lines if it gets him something he wants? He'll do it until one of three things happens. The first is that it gets so risky he walks away. The second is that there's a close call, and that scares him out of it. The third is that he gets caught, and that forces him out of it.

At this point I was just a delivery guy, no more than that. The truly dangerous people wouldn't even know my name. So I chose sides. The potential was there to cross over and join them. As a young man with growing confidence and the fighting skills to back it up, I could do awful things if I chose to. Thank God I never ended up doing any of them, never took a walk too far down that road. With that in mind, I'm glad that, in the end, I got caught. Otherwise it all could have ended with my head blown off. It happened to some of the guys I was in with, and it happened just like that. Boss takes you for a boat ride, then you're a mile off the Florida coast with chains around your ankles, and a coked-up crazy man bends your neck over the bow of his day sailer and ventilates your forehead with a Glock he bought just for the job. It could have happened to me.

I was one of the lucky ones, and by that I mean I came out the other side with my life, and without having to pay the piper every penny he could have demanded. I lost cash and friends and opportunities— a fortune. I felt a lot of pain and fear. But I escaped after having learned the lesson I needed to save my life, then remake my life. I did the whole crash-and-burn thing but somehow escaped the burn. I eventually walked away with my old world in flames behind me, and I never looked back.

But one more time, I'm getting ahead of myself. I'm telling you lessons learned from after the dark part ended, and I've barely told you where it all began.

I took Steve's offer and made the trip with Tonita. For all the intrigue, the trip itself was completely uneventful, meaning it went exactly like it was supposed to. It had all the excitement of driving to the grocery store and back. I pulled up, left the car where they told me, got in another car, and drove back to Steve's place. Going out I was smuggling pot. Coming back I had a car full of money. The difference was night and day: a car full of pot is illegal, but a car with some money in it? Fishy but not against the law.

Steve gave me the five grand in the form of 250 twenty-dollar bills. Bankers call that two and a half "straps," just under five inches of stacked cash and, to a guy like me, a small fortune. All these years later, though, I remember it as something else: stacks and stacks of cash, the kind of thing you'd see in a movie, the kind of cash you pile up on a hotel bed and roll around in. I know it wasn't like that, but memory does funny things. What I see in my memory is how I felt: I was suddenly rich, at least as I counted rich. That feeling was important because it would be the determining factor for many of the decisions I would make in the coming months and years, decisions that would direct the course of my life.

The deal came with one other benefit. You remember how I said I wasn't so good of a student? I was double lousy at math, but this was the beginning of the end of that. Before long I was a numbers whiz. I wasn't doing calculus, but who needs to? I quickly acquired the skills for financial transactions—percentages, fractions, quick counting, that kind of thing. Eventually I would be more fluent with numbers than I am even today with words.

As for the source of Steve's pot, that was a man I hadn't yet met. But the guy would turn out to be the first giant of the twentieth-century drug trade in America. He made a lot of guys broken and broke. A few guys he made rich. Not me. It was my connection to this guy that in only a few years would send me to prison, watching time run out as I tried to bargain my way out of twenty-five to life.

Chapter 7

BODYGUARD

Ray Thompson needed a bodyguard.

As of the 1980s, Raymond Michael Thompson was the biggest marijuana smuggler in American history. In less than a decade, "Little Ray" and his Miami mafia brought a couple million pounds of marijuana into the US and sold it for about a billion dollars in profit, depending on who's talking and how you count. That's a bigger deal than you're thinking. Today in the US there are more than seven hundred billionaires. In the early 1980s there were only a dozen. The billion dollars in pot commerce around Ray didn't all end up in his personal account, but he could take credit for damn near all of that weed making it into the country, and all that profit, no matter who ended up with it.

Next time you're at the airport, sitting at the Southwest Airlines gate and hoping your high-number boarding pass doesn't mean you're stuck with a middle seat, look out the window to see if you can find where the private jets take off. More often than you know, one of the guys in one of those planes is a guy like Ray was—or rather, who Ray could have been. Those people boarding their own private jets—not a rental, but one with their name on the title—those people made it there because, legal or illegal, they conducted themselves professionally.

Ray Thompson could have been the Rockefeller of reefer. Or think Gus Fring on *Breaking Bad*, the ruthless bad guy who treated the drug business as seriously as his legitimate chain of chicken joints, *Los Pollos Hermanos*. Ray was never disciplined enough (or let's be honest, smart enough) to maximize the power and profit of his criminal enterprise. He didn't have it in him. Instead he put all his chips on the part of him that was careless, loud, and violent.

It still blows my mind that it ended the way it did because it didn't have to. He wasn't selling heroin or running machine guns. In those days, most of the market for weed was kids who had to pool their money just to get a dime bag, and that was on a good day. But it wasn't the dealing that got him in the deepest trouble. Ray Thompson ended up on death row as most of its residents do. He was a killer.

"The Little Guy"—that's what people called him when he wasn't around—started out as a small-time loser who got pinched for things like breaking and entering and grand theft auto, the kinds of shortcuts he'd take for the rest of his life. When he found his calling years later in the drug trade, what he did was rarely hands-on crime and, more often, hands-off threats. He was an administrator who only occasionally came out from behind the desk to shoot people in the head. Ray saw himself as the boardroom type, if a boardroom counts as the back office of some storefront like on *The Sopranos*. In Ray's case, he ran things from out behind the Amity Yacht Center on Twenty-First

Avenue in Fort Lauderdale, a basically legitimate boatyard, out in the open. Such was South Florida in the late '70s and early '80s.

Maybe he was so careless because he had no conscience. When I worked in the hospital for the criminally insane, I learned that this is one of the hallmarks of a psychopath. In 1980 Ray ordered the killing of two guys, Robert Vogt and William Harris, over a fight with them at the boatyard. Or consider what he did two years later to his friend of two decades, Jimmy Savoy. Ray took Jimmy onto one of his boats, drove it a half-mile from the beach, wrapped the guy in chains, bent him over the stern side, and shot him in the head.

My brother-in-law Steve introduced us before all that. Maybe he wanted to help me out with more opportunities for cash, maybe he wanted to bring Ray a new resource, maybe he just wanted to show off his family connection to a martial arts champion who was about to win the title. With that $5K drive across the state and back, I'd proven to Steve that I could be trusted, which mattered because Steve knew something else important: Little Ray dealt as much in pot as in trust. I would learn that Ray liked that I was an up-and-coming fighter. He also liked that I was clean. I didn't even swear all that much. I didn't do drugs, didn't drink, didn't smoke—I take care of my body, remember. Later, when I was modeling and did a cigarette ad, they had to show me how to hold it. If Ray trusted you, you were 90 percent of the way with him. But he didn't rely solely on being a good judge of character. When he asked people to do things, it was implicit that they could back up the request with muscle. My ability in that department is what made me a lock.

Most of the time, Ray backed up his demands not with his own fists but by paying other people to beat the shit out of someone or shoot them. That works in the smuggling world. Out in the straight world, though, you need something more subtle, which was pretty ironic for Miami in the 1980s. The place was the opposite of subtle, all loud, garish, and bright. Remember *Miami Vice*? In real life everything was even bigger, brighter, and louder. Cigarette boats, sports cars—Ray liked Corvettes and owned a fleet of them—and models in disco dresses: that was the world Ray moved in. He needed protection he could get not by flashing a gun but by flashing a look. He wanted a guy who could "just say no"—another irony—and whoever or whatever was in the way would step aside.

That's why he chose me to stand next to him at public events, parties, clubs, in the mix for the Miami nightlife. He didn't just want to move in those social circles. He wanted to be at the center. A lot of times, he was. At this point, I was ranked number ten in my weight class. You'd better believe Ray liked having that guy around. He liked it so much that sometimes he paid me just to be around and work out. Five hundred bucks a week and he got the privilege of having a kickboxing champion-in-waiting as his body man across the sex- and drug-drenched South Florida nightclub scene.

He didn't say a word about watching his back while he did business, and that was fine by me. It was only later that I realized that most of Ray's generosity came not because of how he felt about me as a person or as a fighter, but because of how it made him feel to have me around and to be able to count on my loyalty. He figured there was prestige in having the kickboxing champ in his entourage. He was right. But however selfish or selfless the reason, Ray was good to me. He came to my fights, brought dozens of people. When things got wild at his Hendricks Isle party place or anywhere else, he sent me home. He could have used up my good reputation for his own profit, but he didn't. Later, when I asked him to let me in on the operation, he said no. I was the only unspoiled thing in his life, and Ray was desperate to preserve that.

Taking the job at all was a mistake, but it was my mistake, and it didn't feel like that at the time. "You be my bodyguard, then?" he asked. I told him I was in.

Chapter 8

SMUGGLER

Being Ray's bodyguard was good money, but not compared to what I got for that run for Steve. Suddenly I had five grand in my pocket at a time when I was making $7,200 a year. All I'd had to do was make an easy drive to the Gulf and back with my girlfriend. I had one thought: *give me more of that.*

Ray had his operation, the biggest in America, and I had mine. He didn't know what I was doing, and I made sure to keep it that way. It was one more dangerous irony in a lifetime of them: I was the straight-arrow bodyguard for the biggest pot smuggler in history while running my own competing smuggling operation. It was only years later that it really hit me: if Ray had figured me out, it would have been a death sentence, yet I'm still here. Did he like me enough to let it slide, or was he really unaware? I'll never know.

I asked Steve for more runs. He came through. The connections I made introduced me to more guys in this business and more opportunities. Things escalated quickly and profitably. With all those pot runs—drive up with the bundles, come back with the money—you might be wondering where the weed came from in the first place. To tell you the truth, most of the time I didn't know. Jamaica? Could be. The Bahamas? Probably. Central America? South America? Sure, why not? All I knew was that it came through the harbor. That's when I got into the front end of the business, bringing in big-dollar loads of weed on my own boats. I became part of an ongoing smuggling operation that was good enough to fool the Coast Guard, plus whatever agents were in chase at the time.

Bringing drugs into Florida was like any other business. You could succeed if you looked at the problems and figured out a way to solve them. There's lots about the daily operation of the smuggling business you can't hear outside the courtroom or the back room. Here are some of the rules:

Rule #1: Buy a boat. Whoever your supplier is, he's not sailing up to your slip to drop off the packages. You get the coordinates by radio and set off, sometimes no more than a mile or two offshore, sometimes all the way to Jamaica. Point is, you're going to them, not the other way around. Wherever you end up, you'll meet another boat, sometimes big and sometimes small. For me, the typical deal was ten thousand pounds or more, moved from their boat to mine in about two hours. Then you come back to Florida, where you need Rule #2.

Rule #2: Blend in. Most of the boats in the harbor are pleasure boats—fishermen, retirees, folks out for an hour or a day. They're dressed for it, too, and you can see in their faces that they're there for fun. A couple of nervous guys zipping over the horizon only to zip back an hour later? You'll fit in about as well as strippers at midnight mass. But there's a way to fix that: load up your boat with old people. Put fishing poles in their hands. Give 'em blankets for their legs. Hell, bring an oxygen tank or two. You say your girlfriend wants to go? Buy her a nurse's outfit, she'll fit right in, tending to the needs of your golden-age passengers—as cover for your golden opportunity. I was involved in a caper or two where we went all in on the old-folks look, like the time we brought on a guy with no legs! The Coast Guard is looking for shifty-looking guys and marijuana bales, not sleepy retirees reeling in red snapper. Almost every time, they let that kind of boat go right past. If they happen to stop you, take it from me: roll out a guy with no legs and you'll shut down an inspection pretty fast.

Which brings me to my last rule. Sometimes you need more than a good disguise. You need to defy the laws of physics.

Rule #3: Bring the paint. When I first spent time at the marina, I noticed guys doing their bottom-painting more often than they had to and painting them a lot higher than they ought to be. I couldn't figure out why, so one day I asked somebody. The answer is obvious—and pure, simple genius. Smugglers knew how much poundage they were going out to pick up on a given run. They'd load the boat with the amount in sandbags and paint the waterline there. Next they'd sail out, pick up the load, dump the sandbags, and sail back with the waterline the same depth as when they left. The waterline, of course, varies with the load in the boat: the more weight, the lower the boat sits in the water. It mattered because the Coast Guard sometimes took a snapshot of a boat as it left the harbor, then compared the waterlines when the boat came back. If the waterline was too low, they had you. Trade the load for sandbags, though, and your problem is solved.

I made big money fast. In a few months I had saved $50,000 in cash, which I kept in a safety deposit box. Now I had the money I needed for my legitimate goal, to open my own karate school. Jim Martin had moved to Michigan, so I took over his old dojo, Olympic Karate on Pembroke Road, where I had started my martial arts training on my dad's first payment and the encouragement of Mr. Martin himself. I was seventeen.

How did I launder my smuggling money to pay for the karate school? I didn't have to. In those days, you could deposit all the cash you wanted in your local bank, no questions asked. I broke up the $50,000 into smaller deposits, just to be extra careful about not drawing attention. All of a sudden I had legitimate money and could write all the checks I had to. I renamed the place Hollywood Karate. Marketing was a snap: I was a few fights away from the title, so I was three things at once, the owner, the trainer, and the draw. I put in a boxing ring, naturally. I also pitched classes for kids. Karate had been transformative for me. If I could help some other kid like I'd been, I wanted to do it. Years later, helping kids would become a theme in my professional life. This was a solid first round.

Yeah, I know what you're thinking. I'm talking about kids after all this about pot, but hear me out. The smuggling wasn't aimed at kids. It was for adults who wanted marijuana. We hear a lot today about "bodily autonomy"—my body, my choice. If that doesn't apply here, what does? I provided something that adults wanted and, it must be noted, could not hurt them like cigarettes and alcohol do. If I could make money filling the gap, so be it.

I was no big-time smuggler, but I was definitely in the game and gaining an appetite for more. I asked Ray if he would let me join his operation. He said no. As always, he said he wanted me clean.

I didn't tell him I was already in. I couldn't tell him. He would've sent me packing. Hell, he might have hurt me or worse, given how cutthroat he was about competition. But it was more than that. What Ray got from me he couldn't get anywhere else, and he figured the benefit would only get bigger and better. When I got to the top, a little of my clean reputation might rub off on him as the benefactor, employer, and friend of the world champion. Everything he owned had dirt on it. Keeping me clean gave him one more way to look legit.

I remember the conversation. He looked at me like I was something he had never seen up close. Ray was gonna keep me clean as long as he could, at least until he wanted something else, more. That day would come. Not my proudest moment, playing along. If you wanted a reminder of how far there was to fall, all you had to do was look around. A lot of the guys who worked for him were users—pot, cocaine, even heroin, which in most cases was their last stop on their way out of the organization in particular and life in general. I was in this dangerous life, but I was not *of* it. I'm glad I never got used to it. That's a line you don't want to cross.

My life was opposite things at the same time. On one side I was smuggling marijuana. On the other, I was a martial artist who never touched the stuff. I was a disciplined athlete among casually violent men who acted on any impulse that came to mind. If there was an upside to this, it was that I learned to live like that without going crazy. I'm grateful for the lesson and grateful that, in the end, the price I paid to learn it wasn't higher.

Around this time I heard from a guy who asked if I knew anybody who wanted to sell some pot. He wasn't looking to buy a dime bag. He wanted to move significant product. This was the chance I was waiting for, to be the middleman, which is the most profitable (and safest) place to be in one of these transactions. You're dealing with people who've already proved themselves. When he asked, I had the answer already in the chamber.

"Think I might," I said.

This guy, call him Rob, had met me in a stash house in New York. I guess I was the only guy he knew to call. Lucky me, though, because he began buying 1,500 to 2,000 pounds a month. At the time, pot was going for about $220 a pound. I'd buy the order from Steve at $150, who got it from Ray, who had no idea that the squeaky-clean kid he'd turned away from the game was making big money off his own product. He didn't want me in his game, but I was in it anyway. I had become an additional layer in the transaction, meaning I was taking profit he didn't know he was missing. Suddenly I was making thousands more a month.

I did this for years with Rob. Others came around, too. Ultimately, my own crew consisted of my brother, Tony, Scott Errico, and Patrick Bilton. Patrick was a smart kid, younger than me, and owned a couple boats that were moving marijuana full time. His boats were the best boats for smuggling because they had what we called "hidden holes."

In the early days of pot smuggling, you'd load up the boat with as much as five tons and just take a good, hard shot at getting past the Coast Guard. That approach has obvious limits. For instance, the Coast Guard had simply started pulling over more boats, more often. Just making more stops had given them more arrests. But they also got more sophisticated, searching boats for contraband in less-than-obvious places. Which meant smugglers needed places where agents wouldn't think to look, no matter what.

It took six months to build a boat with a hidden hole. Patrick would install the fuel tank as normal, but inside that tank would be a hole leading to a tank within the tank. And the build was so subtle and the hole so hard to spot—and so important to the success of every smuggling run—that only the captain would know it was there and how to access it.

One of the most effective tricks in the Coast Guard's arsenal was to come on board with dogs, drill holes all around, and see if the dogs could smell anything. But they'd never drill a hole anywhere near the fuel tank. Not only would it risk blowing up the boat, but it would also be a waste of time because you can't store anything in a tank filled with gasoline. It hadn't occurred to them that we might hide the stuff in a tank within a tank and use their assumptions against them. The "hidden hole" was the perfect hideaway. Agents wouldn't drill into it and dogs couldn't smell it. The success rate for those boats, mine included, was 100 percent. The plan was brilliant. The only reason I'm telling you the secret now is that I'm not in that business anymore.

Chapter 9

TALKER

I was Ray's bodyguard, still clean as a whistle as far as he knew. I was still working with the cops, teaching self-defense through the police academy. I was teaching a few public classes at the dojo, too. But that didn't add up to much cash. The principal source of my income was the pot business. I had replaced the Alligator Alley income with worlds-better money as a smuggler and middleman, arranging deals with Steve as the supplier and Rob and others as dealers buying from me. We're talking three or four thousand pounds of pot that put twenty-five to thirty grand in my pocket every month.

I had a Mercedes convertible. It was a used one, maybe five years old, and I got it for a song, but all that mattered to me was that it looked cool, and it did. Plus I had my own townhouse where I was living with Tonita. A young man who makes money off karate shouldn't have been able to afford either of those things. That might have drawn attention, but it wasn't as reckless as it sounds. You could live beyond your means and fit in if you aimed for the right crowd, and this was late-'70s/early-'80s South Florida. You saw people living like this all over the place, so much so that it was more a fashion statement than a declaration of wealth. Plenty of people wanted to live this way and look this flashy, and they'd spend their last dime and then borrow more to do it. If you figured someone was doing something illegal, you were the exception if you got worked up about it, let alone tried to get somebody in trouble. Most people running in the neon world of South Florida in those days knew the score. They understood that a lot of things went on outside the law and they didn't ask questions. Besides, you could always come up with a way to explain the opulence and the decadence. It might not be a plausible explanation, but if you wanted to convince yourself it was all good, it was easy. Even the cops mostly looked the other way.

I liked having things, but that wasn't what mattered most. Far more important was that my kickboxing career was heating up. I was ranked in the top five in my weight class worldwide. Heady stuff for me and a big deal in the fight game. Now sports reporters were taking notice. I got a call from the Fort Lauderdale *Sun-Sentinel*. A reporter there wanted to do a story on me.

"I hope you're on the straight and narrow," Joe said to me. He couldn't prove it, but he knew in his heart I wasn't. He was warning me, but he didn't want to confront me, and he didn't want to admit to himself that what looked true was true.

"Everything's fine, Joe," I said. "It'll be a great story for the paper."

"You bet, Ted," he said. "Just don't break my heart."

You know sports reporters. They want to talk about sports. But the fight game is as much about personalities as it is about the athletics. The fight game is part punishing sport, part punishing soap opera, and shocking revelations are the prized stock in trade. When you can find one, you have something big. So reporters go fishing whenever they see half a hint.

This reporter, he said to me, casual as can be, "You have a nice townhouse, Ted. You have a nice car." No secret there, no problem putting that in the paper. All I had to do was nod and agree. Be a little modest. Tell him how I got a deal on the Mercedes—*bought it for a song!* I could have said. That would have been the end of it. But instead of saying thank you, I let my nerves or my pride or something take over the talking.

"Well," I said, dragging it out, "ya know, most people would see all this and think I'm a drug dealer."

A drug dealer? What the fuck was I saying?

"I get it. I have a nice townhouse. I have a nice car." I was like a guy who showed up at his own funeral and starts digging his own grave—*"Hey, everybody! I got a shovel right here. Watch this!"*

I have a townhouse. I have a Mercedes. I look like a drug dealer. That was the big takeaway I gave him. The kindest thing you could say to that was public relations was not my forte.

Here was my attempt to fix it. "At the end of the day, sir, all I do is I work with law enforcement. Plus I train. Plus I fight. All I'm trying to do is become a world champion, the greatest kickboxer in the world."

I did it! I talked my way out of it! Saved! Crisis averted! Except . . . then I said one last thing: "But I get it. Sometimes people think that I'm selling drugs."

They put that into the Fort Lauderdale news. Rather, *I* put that into the Fort Lauderdale news. Thank God they didn't know the rest. The truth is I didn't want to admit how deep in I was. I refused to look around. I didn't know what might come next, but I was about to find out.

Chapter 10

HOSTAGE

Around this time, my friend Patrick Bilton was running one of his boats off of Jamaica when it caught fire with two tons of pot on board. It burned to the waterline and sank, leaving him $300,000 in debt to Jimmy Biggs, head of the Jamaican Defense Force. Jimmy had fronted Patrick the pot "on the arm," meaning Patrick got it without any cash down. This was on the promise that after he'd sold it, he'd come back with the money, and it would be the first round of a long and profitable partnership. Patrick hightailed it the two hours back to Florida and called me.

"I owe Biggs three hundred thousand dollars. Now I can't pay him," said Patrick. "I'm gonna go back down there and explain in person. It'll be fine."

"No, it won't," I said. "You don't have his money, it's gonna be your ass."

"I'm gonna get him to give me another load to sell. Then I'll pay him back for both of them," he said.

"He's not gonna give you another load," I said. "He wants his money. You have the money. Pay him."

Patrick was being cheap, as usual.

"You gotta come with me," he said. "The two of us? He'll be fine with it." I knew it wouldn't work, but I also knew he was walking into trouble so deep that if he went by himself, he'd never make it back. He rented a Learjet and off we both went to Jamaica.

Jimmy knew we were coming without the money. When we landed, what waited for us was beyond scary, and I knew we were in trouble. He had his Jamaican Defense Force guys surround the plane, a ring of jeeps each with machine guns mounted on the roof, each gun with a triggerman behind it. They took us off in cuffs, threw us in a truck, and drove us to the stash house, one of several buildings on Jimmy's compound.

The conversation Patrick wanted wasn't going to happen. Instead, Jimmy and his guys were shouting that they wanted their money, and that was all the talking they'd allow. Before we'd arrived they'd been snorting coke and freebasing, then trying to take the edge off of it with pot. In that state they were gonna do whatever they were gonna do. They were angry before. Now they were angry and high as fuck.

After an hour of this, Patrick somehow got them to understand that he wanted a second load so he could sell it and pay them back for both loads. To show he was serious, he'd even sent a boat ahead to pick it up. They didn't care. They wanted money, only money, nothing else. I knew where this was headed. In an hour or in a day they'd be so tired and so wrecked that they'd stop asking for money and shoot us so they could go home.

They had secured our hands in front of us, the first lucky break of many that day. We weren't going to be able to buy more time, so I had to act fast. There was a ballpoint pen on the table in front of us. I turned my wrists enough to grab the thing. I whispered "On three" to Patrick. We'd flip the table, I'd shoulder tackle the closest thug, jab him in the throat with the pen, grab the gun, and then we'd run. It would work not because we were clever or because I was a martial artist. It would work because these goons were as wasted as a person can be and still remain conscious.

On three, I leaned in. That's when Patrick shouted, "He's got a pen!"

In the history of threats, "He's got a pen!" has to rank right up there with "Watch out for that pillow!" But for these guys, paranoid and stoned, it was enough. I was done before I got started. They grabbed their guns and beat me with them. In that moment I would have been happy to toss Patrick to the wolves. Lucky for him I wasn't going to be the asshole he'd just been. The guys got tired of hitting me, then did some more drugs, I guess to celebrate their victory over the tied-up guy and a blue Bic ballpoint.

It began to get through to these guys that none of what they were doing was going to get them the money they were after. So, finally, they let me speak. "How about I make a phone call? I'll call some guys. They'll send the money over," I said. "You get your money and then you let us go."

"Now we're talking," one said. "You tell your friend to bring the money here, right here," meaning the stash house where they were holding us.

"I said I'd get you the money, but I'm not stupid. If he brings it here, then you'll just take the money and take him hostage, too."

"You have to trust us," said one of the men.

"Are you fucking serious?" I asked. They laughed at that. I guess they knew how dumb it sounded, asking me to trust them like this. "We do it in public. At the hotel."

"We do it here," he said.

"My friends aren't coming to your stash house just so you can kill 'em when they get here. You want your money? I'll get the money. But you have to come get it."

Finally, Jimmy started talking. "This is a trick," he said.

"How's this a trick, Jimmy? You know everything that goes in and out of here."

Jimmy appreciated flattery. "Yes," he said. "I know when everything comes and goes."

"You sure do," I said. "You'll know what we do every step of the way, but to keep us safe, it's always gonna be in public. You take me to the hotel. When they land, your guys take them to the hotel to meet me. You want insurance? Keep Patrick here at the stash house." Patrick shot me a look, but he'd lost the right to question me.

"My guys come inside the hotel. They'll have the money. You gimme some time to count it, okay?" Jimmy was still listening. That was a good sign. "You want me to bring it right here to the stash house, right? We'll drive it here. You give us a car."

"No, Ted. No car."

"What do you think we're gonna do, drive to Florida?"

"Fine," he said. "We'll drive you."

"We're on a fuckin' island, Jimmy. Gimme the fuckin' car." Jimmy thought about it for a moment. I said, "We'll come here. You get the money, we get Patrick. Deal?"

He was quiet for a minute. "Okay," he said. "Let him use the phone."

Chapter 11

ESCAPEE

I called one of my partners, Scott Errico, and told him to put $300,000 in a bag, bring my brother, Tony, and hire a plane. As promised, Jimmy's men took me to the hotel, then handed me the keys to their car. They got in a van with three other guys. This was the crew keeping us honest. They'd lead the way back to the stash house. Scott, Tony, the money, and I would follow in the other car.

Within a couple hours my guys arrived. I passed them a drawing on a napkin. There was more to the plot than Jimmy knew. We'd drive to the stash house as promised, but when we got near the house, the plan would change. We'd let the lead car get out in front of us far enough to lose sight of us for just a few seconds. During that, Scott and I would bail. We'd go on foot the rest of the way, hiding in the sugarcane and corn while Tony continued the drive. Instead of delivering the two of us with the cash, he'd honk the horn and drive back and forth, like he expected someone to come out and tell him what to do. When someone finally did come out, Scott and I would knock him out, retrieve Patrick, and jump in with Tony. He'd floor it to the water. Eddie, who had been hiding out on the island after the original fire at sea that caused all this, would captain us out on the boat Patrick had planned to use for the second load that wasn't coming.

Scott had added something of his own to the plan: two guns he'd tossed in with the cash. We each took one, but he warned me not to fire. All it would take was one gunshot. We figured Jimmy's men nearby would hear it and come running with guns of their own.

"The last thing I'm gonna do is pull a trigger," I said. "Let's just get this done."

It all went according to plan except that Tony got there faster than it took us to cross the fields. That meant he ended up honking that horn longer than it made sense. Finally one of Jimmy's men came out a side door and waved at him to come on in. Tony didn't acknowledge him. Instead he kept driving back and forth. That's when the guy knew something was up. We were still thirty yards away when he looked in our direction. Scott, who just fucking told me not to take a shot, took a shot anyway.

The guy ducked back in the house, probably to grab his own gun, but it was too late to stop us. We covered the distance and burst in. I grabbed him and slammed him to the floor. Across the room, Jimmy's wife watched the whole thing, dumbstruck. "You see this, Jimmy?" I shouted at him. "Don't you fucking surprise me!" I took her with me from room to room, clearing the house. Patrick was nowhere. They had gone back on the deal and taken him away, probably to make it easier to take the money and kill us all. Maybe they'd already killed Patrick. Everything was on the table.

Now Jimmy emerged. I pushed him into a bedroom and sat him down next to his wife. "All I want is my friend. Where is he?" I said. I pointed my gun at his forehead. "You get one chance."

Jimmy didn't hesitate. "The mansion."

The mansion was Jimmy's own palace, his big, garish headquarters, a poor man's idea of how a rich man lives. I handed Jimmy the phone. "Call up there. Say you're sending someone to get Patrick, and your wife is coming with him." I kept my gun on Jimmy, turned my eyes to her. "You're not back in fifteen minutes, you know what happens." I told Tony to make the short drive to the mansion and bring Patrick back. Jimmy's wife would go along for insurance.

Minutes after they left, somebody was at the door. Not Jimmy's cavalry. They couldn't know what was going on and they wouldn't knock if they did. Too much time had passed for this to be a response to Scott's stupid gunshot. What the fuck was going on?

Turned out Jimmy had left out a big detail—not a deadly detail, just something even Jimmy might forget at a time like this. When we first busted in, I knew the mound of coke and all those straws I saw were too much for just a handful of guys, and I had been right. This crazy scene hadn't been just a hostage welcoming committee; this was a party, and we were early. His side men were coked up because they had been pre-gaming long before we got there.

Big-man Jimmy had invited about twenty of his friends for the main event. He'd told them to come at the end of the day, and that was now. People started arriving. I started greeting them.

"Come on in!" I'd yell, then swing the door open. Before they could figure out something was wrong, Scott or I would grab them, zip-tie their hands and feet, and toss them on the floor. Jimmy was supposed to be the host, but now we were, and I guarantee it was the shittiest party any of them had ever been to. They'd bang on the door and get yanked in, tied up, and put down. We were stacking his guests like cordwood. They didn't enjoy it but I sure as hell did.

Jimmy's wife and Tony returned with Patrick on time and as ordered. Scott had been drinking and it showed. He had been a fugitive for a while now. He used the alcohol to beat the stress. That's probably why he did what he did next. Scott started grabbing handfuls of cocaine from the table and throwing it at the guests on the floor. "Look at you!" he shouted, throwing the powder into their Jamaican faces. "You gonna turn white, now! You like that?" He marched around the room, laughing, shouting at them, stepping against their bodies.

With the coke suddenly everywhere, some of them saw their chance—not to get away but to start getting high. Being zip-tied didn't stop them a bit. Jimmy's party guests, such as they were, started wiggling around to get closer to the stuff, craning their necks to snort up the shit all over the floor.

Scott threw another fistful. "You want some more coke, motherfucker?" Thing is, they *did* want more coke. They didn't even mind snorting it off the floor while Scott cursed at them. After all, they came there for a drug party.

"Knock it off, Scott. We gotta go right now," I urged him. He threw a little more, yelled a little more, danced a little more. I grabbed him, shook him. "Enough!" That brought him back.

We got in the car Jimmy had given us and headed for the water. Tony was at the wheel, Jimmy's wife in the middle, Patrick on the passenger side. In the back it was Scott on one side and me on the other with Jimmy in between. "When we get to the gate you tell the guard it's all good," Scott said to Jimmy. "You try anything, we'll kill you." Biggs did as ordered. It looked fishy but the guard did as he was told.

Now came the last step. It was one thing to come through the gate with the boss, something else to frog-march him onto a boat. We needed a distraction. "Tony," I said, "when I say go, drive it straight into the water, then we all break for the boat. Biggs, you're coming with us. You try to get away, you know what happens."

Now Tony spoke up. "This doesn't go straight to the water. We're at least six feet above it."

"Go anyway," I said.

My brother, now the hero of the piece, got us there and then some. He floored it so hard, it pulled us against our seats. We sailed off the cliff, through the air, over the bay, and hit the water like a brick wall. That's because we crashed into a fucking sandbar. The hood crumpled and all four doors flew open. It's a wonder the car didn't explode. The trunk popped open, too, revealing our bag of money. The goons at the gate looked right past us. I guess they figured if Biggs wasn't yelling for help, they were wise to pretend nothing was happening. They knew better than to ask questions. Jimmy being in the middle of weird shit like this was par for the course.

"Grab the money!" I shouted at Tony.

He was on his belly, flailing. "Fuck the money, man! I'm not gonna drown for that!"

"Stand up, you idiot," I said. He tried, succeeded, and we both started to laugh. We were in two feet of water, still on the sandbar.

Now the three of us, plus Jimmy, waded to the boat. As promised, Eddie was waiting. He turned us for international waters, five miles out. We'd gone no more than a mile when Scott and Patrick told me to dump Biggs off the side. I said no. "If there's trouble, he's our only ticket out of here." I had him bound like we'd done for his party guests at the stash house, zip-tied at the hands and feet and laid across the bow. He wasn't going to be a problem. But his men were.

In that moment, we took a stream of 20 mm machine-gun fire along the starboard side. It was Jimmy's men from the Jamaican Defense Force. These motherfuckers had a cannon, military shit, the kind of thing you mount on a tank. Eddie raised them on the radio. "We have Jimmy Biggs. Do not fire on us. You can see him on the bow." Biggs lay there petrified and trembling, as scared as he'd ever be in his life.

Now Eddie shouted, "Port side!"

It was a US Coast Guard helicopter, arriving with action-movie timing. They kicked on their loudspeaker and turned toward the Jamaican cruiser. "This is the United States Coast Guard. If you shoot at this US boat again, we will fire on you." Never before or since had a smuggler been so happy to see the Coast Guard. Eddie radioed them, identified us, and told them we were headed to Florida. They got on the loudspeaker again. "If you fire again on this US vessel, we'll blow you out of the water. Let them navigate into international waters." The Jamaicans pulled back, then followed us until we were all out of Jamaican territorial waters, the chopper staying over us. I dragged Jimmy to the stern and hung him over the side. I cut the zip ties, then kicked him into the water.

"So long, you son of a bitch." His goons cruised the short distance over at idle speed so as not to overwhelm their boss, then fished him out of the water.

The Coast Guard came aboard to sort all this out. Of course we played dumb. They found the money and asked where it came from. "Beats me," I said. "I bet it belonged to that guy in the water." Whatever they believed, they had no jurisdiction in international waters.

All they could do is what they had to do: tow us to the nearest safe port, the Cayman Islands, and give us over to the local authorities. We were in the home stretch, no longer subject to the coked-up whims of Jimmy Biggs and the by-the-book rules of the Coast Guard. Now all we had to contend with was the usual, expensive Caribbean bullshit.

Before we even got there, we knew what the deal would be: they'd keep the $300,000 and our slightly shot-up, $400,000 boat. In exchange, we'd get to leave. It wasn't much of a deal, but considering how the day had gone, I was glad to be breathing.

Chapter 12

BUSINESSMAN

Ray ran a smuggling business. My partners and I ran a smuggling business. That's what we had in common. We differed on a whole lot more.

Everything with Ray was a transaction: cash, ass, or grass. He was running a fucking mob out of the boathouse, sitting at the top of a 24/7 enterprise with a hundred employees on hand, even more connections around the world, and an operation moving hundreds of millions of dollars in product a year. They even had a kind of logo, a little inside joke, a gold ring marked with the shape of a marijuana bud and seeds. If you saw somebody wearing one of those, you'd know it was one of Ray's guys. But Scott, Patrick, and me? We weren't going for world domination. We were freelancers in it to make as much money as we could, while we could, and we were making a ton of it. We were friends, we looked out for each other, and we could trust each other.

When Ray needed something he couldn't do himself, he had guys all around him who could take care of it. When we needed something we couldn't do, we had to expand the circle. Fortunately, there was no shortage of upstanding Miami-area citizens with a little money or ambition eager to try their hand in our illegal, high-profit game. When our business grew to the point that we could no longer process the cash on the fly, we set up a permanent location for the work. A friend and I, we'll call him Mike, secured a pair of beautiful condos on the bay, just over the Rickenbacker Causeway. These condos sat one on top of the other. We had about fifteen counting machines in there, and when times were busy, we'd work twenty-four hours a day, sorting millions of dollars in bills. We were accountable for getting that money to the people we owed, including offloaders, boat captains, and various others on the take who made sure connections got made at the appointed time with no surprises. What was left was our take, split among the partners. Big money, good times.

For us, business was business and fun was fun. Ray, on the other hand, looked for a chance to make money in everything, even the parties. He had a party house that put any other to shame. Las Olas Boulevard in Fort Lauderdale is a major route through the city, and in those days it was being transformed into a destination for shopping and nightlife. It had long been home to celebrities, too. Connie Francis kept a place there, as did Lucy and Desi, Sonny and Cher, Gloria Vanderbilt, and plenty of other celebrities and big-dollar CEOs. Naturally, Ray put his party house there, and he made sure it was the biggest. This place was six huge apartments combined into one, a luxury location with a view of the water, complete with his own seventy-foot sailboat lightly bobbing just outside and decked-out hot tubs all around. As for the entertainment, this place was ground zero for Pretty People

Disease. Every woman was gorgeous, every man came in the door loaded down with cash and drunk on his own swagger, and every drug flowed freely: coke, pot, sometimes more adventurous assholes shooting heroin. This was Ray's party place for all the smugglers.

But like I said, he didn't put on this spread to congratulate the other smugglers with good dope and a nice view. Ray had an angle. The party house was a way to bring traffic into his own high-dollar brothel, a portable outfit he called The Little Devils. Guys would descend on the place after a big run, pockets full of money to spend, and you can write the rest of that story. There'd be a couple dozen beautiful girls there, and you could have any one you wanted for a thousand bucks a night. With the drugs and drink flowing freely, it was an easy sell.

I was there pretty often, but never for the party. I was a smuggler, too, even if Ray didn't know it, but I was still his bodyguard. This event was one the things he hired me for, to be the guy he could count on to stay straight in the middle of a drugged-out scene. I saw lots of these parties go down as I kept an eye on Ray's safety. He had his business; I had mine.

When my guys got together to work, we tried to keep things strictly business. Sometimes things got dangerous when we least expected it. Sometimes it was the fault of one of us; sometimes it was just fate. One day Scott and I were at the Omni at the Star Island Resort on Biscayne Bay. We'd set up a perch a safe distance away to watch ten thousand pounds of marijuana be offloaded from our boat. Scott was a fugitive at the time. He wasn't always careful, and sometimes we couldn't save him from himself. This day he had been drinking—too much, I thought. We got in an elevator and I said something about it.

"Scott, lay off the sauce," I said. "We have business going on. I need you straight."

"Yeah?" he said. "What are you going to do about it?"

That was all it took. We grabbed each other and started going at it as the elevator rose higher and higher. No punches, just a scuffle. Then Scott drew a pistol and brought it to my face. I grabbed his hand. He pulled the trigger. The shot went through the elevator wall. He nearly shot my fucking head off.

A second later, the elevator stopped on our floor, opening into a mercifully empty hallway. We fell out, ears ringing, and went in opposite directions. In any other business, that would have been, at best, the end of a friendship. But in our business, it was just another weird day at the office.

Another deal took us to New England. We brought a tugboat carrying thirty thousand pounds of pot into Boston Harbor. To get clearance into the port, we had to bribe the local mob guys fifty grand. Pat, Scott, and I made a nice score. A couple months later we tried it again, but we made our move before we'd settled with the Massachusetts mobsters. Based on what happened next, I guess our credit wasn't good with them.

About twenty of us were piled into the back of a huge rental truck headed to the harbor when the agents pulled us over, obviously on a tip from the guys we hadn't paid off. Of course, the truck was empty, since we were on the way to the harbor to offload. But in this game, the agents can always find a way to haul you in, especially when they might be in cahoots with the guys who sent them your way in the first place.

There'd be no way a few officers could catch twenty men going in every direction, so we knew our best bet was to scatter. As soon as they opened the back of the truck, I hit the lead cop in the jaw, he hit the floor, and every guy inside came flying out. I'd never seen racehorses out of the hole going faster than these guys.

But not fast enough. Nearly everybody got caught. Scott and I got away, though, and spent the night sleeping in a doghouse.

Chapter 13

FALL GUY

The beginning of the end came on the afternoon of Wednesday, June 24, 1981. I can divide my life into everything that came before that day and everything after.

I think Ray knew that law enforcement was closing in. If you're a big-time dealer, it's smart to be a little paranoid, but in this case he was right. That said, the last thing you need is to add to it. Ray was deep into the coke. A lot of the guys around him were messed up, too. Plus Ray had no way of knowing if they were working for him alone, for themselves, for a rival, or for the Feds. He started running out of people he could count on.

I was the only guy in his circle who didn't do drugs and, as far as he knew, I wasn't in the smuggling game. For years those had been things he had preserved. But as things got dark, they made me one of the few people he could still trust.

"You always wanted to make money," he said.

"Whaddya have in mind?"

"Ted, my friend, your opportunity is right fucking now."

Ray's usual system was to bring in a shipment of pot by boat, maybe forty thousand pounds in a single delivery. He'd move it onto trucks, then send those trucks to stash houses. The switch happened in a matter of hours, and that was the point: never leave it somewhere long enough to be discovered. The rule was to keep it moving, but Ray had been breaking that rule. Now he'd gotten his ass in a crack. The last shipment, he'd had his boys stack the stuff in the boatyard and leave it. Hundreds of thousands of dollars of pot were just sitting there. Bad move. Day in, day out, regular people who went out to fish and ski had free run of the place where they rented a little space. Though they couldn't see into Ray's rental, the smell of pot inside there during that hot summer was obvious.

He needed to get as much product as possible out of there fast. My brother-in-law Steve had a buyer and told Ray I could be trusted to make the delivery—if Ray was willing to part with keeping me "pure." From what I understood, Ray was so high so much around this time that he didn't quite get that the driver was me, which is probably why he made the offer in the first place. Ray would pay me $20,000 for moving fifteen hundred pounds. This was loaded with irony, because my first job for Ray would be the same kind of job I had done to get into the business in the first place, driving product from Point A to Point B. One more irony: this load was going to Rob, who was one of my own guys.

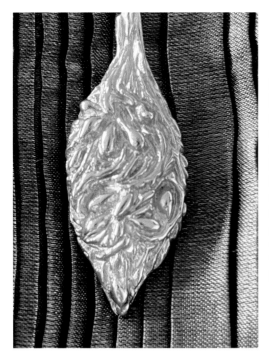

Most of my pictures are from my kickboxing days and not from my other early business, for obvious reasons. In fact, this is just about the only one I have related to "the business." It was an (unwritten) tradition that members of a given smuggling operation would carry an item of custom jewelry that showed you were "inside." This was from my team. The small "globs" of gold represented the bud of the marijuana plant.

Madison Square Garden: I'm throwing a left jab into Greg Straub.

Miami Beach: Fighting Harold Roth, one of the top fighters from Europe. I knocked him out in round three.

Don "The Dragon" Wilson and I teaching an all-women's karate class. That's one way for a single guy to meet women, eh?

Here I am winning first place for non-contact karate matches in middle and light heavyweight divisions—on the same night. With me is John Pachivas, known in my world as the "Father of Florida Karate."

Chuck Norris believed in me early on. On a few things we were even rivals! One thing was always true, though: if somebody's taking a picture of Chuck, everybody within a hundred feet is gonna run over there to get in it, too. Not sure who else is here, but you recognize Chuck, and I'm on his right. This was from 1978, my first pro fight, which Chuck refereed.

A moment from one of my many tournaments. I remember this one. I won.

A kick from me for Ray McCallum.

See the pads on my hands and arms? That's standard equipment for light- or no-contact competition.

You know me. In the middle it's Randall "Tex" Cobb, better known as a boxer and an actor in the end, but early on he was a fine martial artist. On the right, Tonita Queen, first my girlfriend and later my wife, and forever my wonderful friend.

Kicker: me. Kickee: Jack Ballard.

A body shot against Steve Mackie.

Warming up!

My kick. Eugene York on the other end.

Look closely. That's me in the air executing a spinning crescent kick—about 30 degrees into a 360-degree spin. What you can barely see is the stunt we were pulling: that's a cucumber I just knocked loose, barely visible on the right side of my head.

The big night for all the marbles. Las Vegas. Steve Mackie. My fight for the world title. This night I would not be denied.

Me swinging. Mackie in the ropes. The fight goes on!

Pryor with an uppercut to Mackie!

Another big kick from Pryor!

The winner and new champion, Ted Pryor! That's my father matching me with his fists, and my brother Tony smiling between us. What a night!

My night. My belt. My victory. At long last.

That night I was the champ. But every day my brother Tony remains my hero.

Winning over Greg Strong.

Me on the right, with Tony right next to me. My brother, my best friend.

He was the Greatest! We were in Hong Kong and I was fighting that night. Muhammad Ali was there, and what an attraction he was. When they asked him who he wanted to win, he had his answer at the ready: the Champ liked Ted. "I'm pulling for the white boy!" he said. That's an endorsement I'll take.

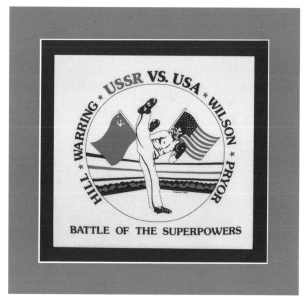

Big excitement in Palm Beach. It was Americans versus Russians— champs against champs. But don't worry: we swept every division.

More good times with the incomparable Chuck Norris, center. That's me on the right, of course, and Jim Martin on the left. Jim was my first sensei. I owe him a lot.

K and G Cinema Development

presents

"CRYSTAL BLUE PERSUASION"

TWO FT. LAUDERDALE COPS, BOTH SKILLED MARTIAL ARTIST, THE ULTIMATE CARIBBEAN DIVING VACATION, AN EXOTIC ISLAND BEAUTY, MILLIONS IN UNCUT BLUE SAPPHIRES, THE ADVENTURE OF A LIFE TIME. . . . . .

Executive Producer
JOE KANTER

Producer - original story:.
RANDY GRINTER

principal photography begins
September '88

K & G Cinema Development
Miami, Florida (305) 576-4310

That's me behind the sunglasses, Joe Hess on the right. Who's that lady? All I know at this date was that she was lovely—and perfect for our movie.

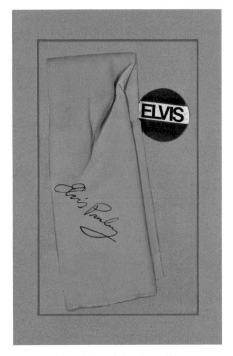

A gift from Elvis himself.

The return of the champ!

Glory days.

TED PRYOR

The classic action shot. That's the good life in kickboxing, isn't it? Executing a perfect kick to the heavy bag in my own gym. Good times.

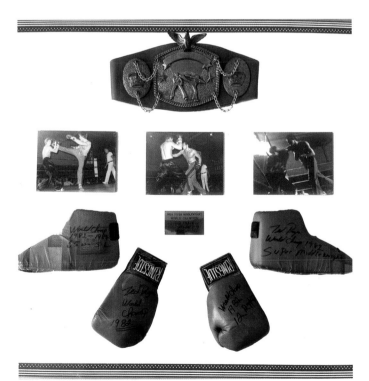

Championship days: the belt, the gear, the photos . . . the memories.

That's me today. The champ's still standing.

The temperature was in the low seventies under a cloudy sky. Steve was standing on security duty in front of the marina. The van was fully loaded. He waved me out of the driveway.

As soon as I turned onto the street, a Camaro came shooting out of nowhere and stayed right on my bumper. I took a left, then a block or two later I made a right. So did the Camaro. This guy showed up so quick and stayed on me so close that there was no doubt he knew what was up. I knew better than to head for the destination, and going back to the marina didn't seem like the smart play, so I drove around the streets near the marina, headed nowhere, hoping for the laws of probability to overcome reality. Maybe this guy just happened to be going the same way I was. Maybe he liked looking at vans. Hell, I'd take any crazy reason if this asshole in the Camaro would just go in some other direction.

I turned onto Davie Boulevard. I'll never forget the name because that's the street where my life changed forever.

As soon as I made the turn, the Camaro shot around in front of me and blue lights came up behind me. *I'm done. Fried. I got fifteen hundred pounds of pot in the truck.*

They pulled me over. They told me to get out of the truck. I did, and locked eyes with an officer I knew.

"Oh my God. It's Ted Pryor."

Yep. Joe Hess's boy. The one who trained that cop, the one who trained nearly all of them. The one who'd always been one of the good guys. The one they'd counted as "one of us." That's who climbed out of a van filled with marijuana.

In that moment, though, our connection counted for nothing. They drew their guns, just like out of a cop show on TV. "Be careful with him," said one. "It's Ted." Whether they meant "be careful" because they didn't want to hurt me, or because I could easily hurt them, would remain an open question for only a few more seconds.

They told me to put my hands against their car. They told me not to move. They threatened to put a bullet in my head. The next thing I heard was something they'd said before, but then it had been in admiration. Now it was in anger and with a little trepidation. "We know you're a lethal weapon."

At least they respect who they're dealing with, is what I thought. "C'mon, guys. I'm not doing anything."

I trained most of these guys. We were friends. But now none of that mattered. They were devastated. So was I. It showed on everybody's faces as they handcuffed me and tossed me in the back of a squad car like anybody else.

They unloaded me at the Fort Lauderdale police station. At first I'd only been handcuffed. Now they shackled my feet. They had already been surprised to find out it was me. I guess they didn't want any more surprises, didn't want to find out if I would put them on the receiving end of what they knew I could do. Or maybe they wanted to protect me from myself, to stop me from doing something stupid and kicking their asses across the parking lot or making them pull a trigger. Thank God we both knew better. As humiliated and angry as I was, I'm grateful that they didn't give me the chance to act on it.

Now it was time for the interrogation. From the moment they knew who they had, they'd been planning this. They knew intimidation wasn't going to work with me, so they went with the old "good cop, bad cop" approach. In case you don't know, it's just like in the movies, or the true crime shows all over TV just now. One guy comes in and reads you the riot act, then he tag-teams out for another guy, slick and sweet, and that guy offers you a can of soda or a cup of coffee and a kind word. He might even talk down the other guy. "No need for that hard stuff," he'll say. "We can talk, man to man," figuring you'll repay the relief with a little cooperation or even a confession. Anyway, that's what they did to me, and they kept it up for six hours.

A couple rounds in, Bad Cop came in one more time, screaming and yelling. No surprise there, but now he had a phone book in his hand, and he made it clear he'd like to beat me with it. This isn't a scene from a movie. This is real life, and the guy is making like he's gonna use my ass for a piñata while I can't fight back.

Like hell I can't fight back. I stood up. "If you think you're gonna hit me with that and walk away, you're sadly mistaken."

Consider the scene: my feet are shackled and I'm handcuffed behind my back. What was I gonna do to this guy? Yet he backed down. He was making a threat he wasn't ready to back up. I may not have had my hands and feet free, but the sternness in my voice made it clear that this was a bad idea in a thousand ways. He was gonna walk into a buzzsaw of a fight with a shackled man who fights for a living. He didn't know what was coming—truth is, neither did I—but it was going to be painful for both of us, plus whoever came in to break it up.

"I'm not gonna hurt you," he says. "You can sit down." So I did. He walked over to the table, sat down across from me, and just like that, the Bad Cop turned into the Good Cop. He was a lieutenant; I won't mention his name here. But we had a few things in common, including working in the same circles in the Fort Lauderdale police department. After he retired, he went on to be a bodyguard for billionaire Wayne Huizenga, who owned Blockbuster Video and AutoNation plus most of South Florida's sports teams: the Dolphins, the Panthers, the Marlins. But that was still in the future.

"Ted," he said, "I can't believe it's you. You know, you were one of us. You've been training the guys who enforce the law. How did you get yourself into this?"

I felt that little pull. *Tell him.* Everything he said was true. I was on the side of the law. These guys had been my friends. I'd been training them so that when things got twisted, they could save their own lives. I had been working for law enforcement and in support of the law itself. I believed in what they stood for —what *we* stood for—and had done together. In that moment, the attraction was real.

Tell him. He deserves to know. He's my friend. He's just trying to help me.

"Tell me who you work for," he said. "C'mon, Ted. So I can get you out of this."

That's when my deeper instinct kicked in. The lieutenant may have been my friend before. In his mind, he was acting like my friend right there. He may even have been telling the truth when he said he wanted the best for me. But what he wanted more than any of that was to put me down, to get the guys I was working for, and if the price of that was putting me in jail—hell, if it meant putting me under the jail—then that's a price he would have been happy to pay. Correction: it's a price he would have been happy for *me* to pay.

This wasn't some friendly conversation, some come-to-Jesus meeting. This was still Good Cop, Bad Cop. As I was rebounding from the Bad Cop routine, I had almost fallen for the Good Cop trick, just as he had planned. He'd played his cards. Now I'd play mine. "I can't tell you anything. I speak to you? I'm a dead man."

They play it for melodrama in the movies, but in real life it's the real thing, the code of silence. I had to stay shut up whether I wanted to or not. If I talked, I'd be dead in a day.

It wasn't a long conversation after that. They knew me well enough to know that hanging around haranguing me wasn't going to break me. All they'd get was a few overtime hours they wouldn't get paid for anyway. So they sent me to lockup. I departed the station in shorts, flip-flops, and a Mickey Mouse T-shirt.

Chapter 14

OFFENDER

Next day, Ray arranged to have my bail paid. "You're going to be fine," he said. "We're going to get you out of this and we're going to clear your name." He really did want me to get out of jail, but not because he gave a damn about me. Ray didn't want me rolling on him. In this case, bail was cheaper than murder, though he was capable of either one. Ray was so desperate to keep anyone he knew from talking to the cops that he didn't stop to realize that I had very little to tell. The stuff I did for Ray was almost always legal, and he kept me out of his business in the first place. All I could give them was second-hand stuff. Hell, it was a sure thing law enforcement knew more than I did. My first illegal job for him had taken place less than twenty-four hours before, and we all know how far that got.

It was my own smuggling business that I wanted to protect, but that's not why they'd arrested me. The cops didn't know my operation even existed.

Ray got me an attorney, a guy named Dohn Williams. These days he's a well-known name, one of the best in Florida, but back then he was still climbing the ladder. Ray said he was the best guy for me. I was no expert on lawyers, so I took who he offered. I was in no position to argue.

The best guy, period, was Steadman Stahl, but he was already working for Ray, so that was a nonstarter. Why? If it ever came down to me versus Ray, it was gonna be Ray every time. Steadman worked out of an office in Hollywood, Florida, under another attorney, Joe Varon. That guy was world famous. If you were a gangster, a hood, a killer, or accused of being any of those things, Joe was your man. And if you couldn't get Joe, you could go with someone who worked for him, a murderer's row, pardon the joke, of criminal-defense talent. That's how I ended up with Dohn. Ray said he was the best.

Why didn't Ray just have me killed? Here's what I think.

The stories about Ray's meting out sloppy, sudden, and cruel violence are legion. If you were in trouble because of something he did, he'd fix it by fixing you. One time Ray welshed on paying his end of a drug deal with some Colombians. For anybody else, that might have been the end of the line, but when it comes to drug dealers, the bottom line is always money. Ray had plenty of that, and he wasn't cheap. Ray was their hostage but somehow talked these cutthroat Colombians into letting him bring in a replacement. The deal was simple, and a bit of an echo of the one we proposed to Jimmy Biggs: *I'm the boss and only I can get the money. Hold my man as collateral while I bring it back.* They bought it and let Ray walk out, keeping one of his men as the new hostage. The difference between his deal and ours is that Ray never came back. He went home and resumed his normal life. Ray didn't give a damn about getting his guy back, even if all it would have taken was the payoff. What became of the replacement hostage, Ray's own man who trusted him with his life? Your guess is as good as mine.

Another time, Ray had a stash of marijuana in a house on Hendricks Isle, a tiny strip of land that's a true island in Fort Lauderdale proper, and a pretty nice place. Somebody stole the bales. Ray was furious. He decided the thief was one of his own men, so he hired a polygraph examiner to come to his headquarters to question everybody who worked for him. As each suspected thief came out of the exam room, the petrified polygraph operator would signal out the window, thumbs up or thumbs down, indicating a pass or fail to Ray, who was sitting outside.

Why wasn't Ray in the room to see the exam for himself? Because he had set himself just beyond the door with a machine gun on his lap, ready to settle the matter with some cartel justice when the offender was identified. Everybody passed the test. Whether that was because they were all innocent or because the examiner gave everybody a thumbs-up to avoid witnessing a massacre—as I said, your guess is as good as mine.

Now I was in Little Ray's sights and expecting the same compassion, so to speak. I was under arrest for rolling out of his headquarters with just short of a ton of pot. Any other day he might have invested in a couple bullets instead of lawyers and bail. But within twenty-four hours of what happened to me, something happened to him.

The day after I was arrested, cops descended on the Amity Yacht Center with a search warrant. They walked out with more than twenty-five thousand pounds of marijuana that had been stored there, plus the other ton in the van. This was the bust that gave investigators the "intent to distribute" charge that later ended up as part of Ray's federal RICO charges, and it was a big deal for every law enforcement agency that had any jurisdiction. All eyes were now on Ray, and if any potential informer suffered so much as a stubbed toe, they'd have pinned it on Ray before the sun had gone down. The Amity bust on June 25 put Ray in the limelight from then on. Though I'll never know for sure, that may have made the difference, literally, between life and my own murder.

For better or worse, the wheels of the justice system turn mighty slow. It would be nearly a year before I came to trial. Dohn was setting me up for the best possible outcome, and these legal maneuvers pushed the start date from September to November, then into January and finally to late March 1982. I was free on bail during all this, so my life went on pretty much as it had before, with my martial arts career on one side—I was getting closer and closer to a title bout—and, on the other side, the smuggling runs with Patrick and others.

After my arrest and the raid that followed, Little Ray's Florida mafia was pretty much out of business. I kept my distance. I'd never been in deep with him anyway, so it wasn't difficult to stay away. But we would have one more significant encounter.

Chapter 15

SURVIVOR

In the same month of my arrest, Ray hired his old friend Jimmy Savoy to build a safe in Savoy's own workshop and gave him just shy of $600,000 in cash to hide there. But Jimmy saw that things were heating up and figured he was too close to avoid the flame. Here's how it looked to me: Jimmy decided that the smart play was to disappear, taking Ray's cash with him. With Ray so distracted and stressed out, he figured he could get away with it. So, he pried open that safe, bought a sports car with some of Ray's money, and fled to North Carolina with the rest—just over a half-million.

It didn't take long for Ray to notice that Jimmy was gone. A quick trip across town revealed that cracked-open safe, and that sealed it: Jimmy had ripped him off.

Ray was pretty hard to surprise, but it's a fair bet that he hadn't seen this coming. Ray and Jimmy had been friends since the 1960s, when Ray first moved to Miami. Jimmy was an ex-jockey and made a little money building tack boxes: storage lockers for horse-riding gear. The two had been partying pals ever since.

Once Ray hit it big, the party hit a new level. Ray's appetite for cocaine rose with his income, and everybody knew his reputation just by seeing him in the club. Hell, as his bodyguard in those places, I saw it up close. Nearly every story about Ray is colored in with insane things he did while he was high, which, toward the end, was nearly all the time except when he was on a boat—he thought being high on one of his boats would undermine him with the crew and look suspicious, besides. Beyond the stories swapped among those who were there, a guy named Eric Sande wrote a short book, *The Real King of Miami,* that shed a little light on Ray's personal life. According to that account, Ray coked up in the morning, stayed awake for days, and went to sleep on a handful of quaaludes. Sometimes he'd hang with Jimmy in the workshop where he'd eventually have that safe, and the two would listen to police scanners and drink beer.

The most important thing Jimmy did for Ray was to rig the boats with secret storage spaces, the same way Patrick had done for our boats: the compartments were so wrapped up in the fuel system that the cops couldn't drill into the load to find it and dogs couldn't smell it.

Now Jimmy was gone. It was a personal insult to Ray, defiance after years of loyalty, a brazen "fuck you" to the guy who'd kept him financially afloat while he scraped by living behind a Burger King in his own workshop.

Ray put his most trusted goons on a serious search for Savoy. They started at the racetracks, where the two had first met and where Ray figured Jimmy was most likely to hide out. Nobody there seemed to know anything. They couldn't have, because the story of Jimmy Savoy was playing out eight hundred miles north.

By September, Jimmy was broke, but not because he'd burned through the cash. He had driven to North Carolina and started partying—on Ray's cash, like before, but stolen, not earned. One night Jimmy called a prostitute, got drunk, and passed out alongside her. The next morning, the woman was gone and so was the money. Now exhausted, broke, and paranoid, Jimmy was certain that Ray had a team of hit men after him. With no friends to call and no place to go, Jimmy presented himself to the FBI and told his story.

I gotta tell you, I don't think that part's true. That Jimmy went to the FBI comes from what a Florida law enforcement agent told the *Sun-Sentinel* three years later, in 1985. C'mon. The FBI heard this story from Jimmy and let him go anyway? Bullshit. He was a rock-solid informant from the inside who could help put Ray away forever, and he gave them separate grounds to keep him around by confessing to a crime. They let him go? Please. Even a receptionist at the front desk would have grabbed the handcuffs and said, "Wait here."

At this point, Jimmy Savoy was as low as he'd ever been, but he still hadn't reached rock bottom. And this is where I reenter the picture.

Maybe he was desperate. Maybe he was tired of waiting. Maybe he was afraid. Whatever he was feeling, Little Ray would now kick things into high gear: it was time to find Jimmy, no more excuses. Around the end of the year, he called a meeting at one of his homes and brought in some of his associates: Patrick Menillo, Bobby Sheer, Bobby "Vegas," Leonard Finestone, and assorted others considerably further down the ladder, including me.

"Quit fucking around," said Ray. "I want this guy right fucking now. Whatever it takes. He ripped me off for six hundred thousand. Bring him here."

Smuggling is one thing. This, what Ray was asking—this was something else. "Ray," I said, "what are you gonna do when you get him?" He looked at me like I was an idiot.

"What do you think I'm gonna do?" he said. Then he popped that awful question, asking me if I wanted to do the hit.

I'm proud to say what I did next came as pure reflex. "I'm out," I said, and I stood up to leave. "I'm not grabbing anybody, I'm not killing anybody, not for stealing six hundred grand, not for four million or whatever number. I'm not killing anybody."

"You fucking pussy fuck," Ray said. He tore into me with insults, and he didn't let up except to take a breath. None of the guys in the room dared stand up for me or against him.

"I'm telling you, Ray," I said, "I'm not killing anybody."

The threats continued, and after another minute or two of this, it started to feel like Ray was going to practice on me what he intended to do to Jimmy Savoy. I stood my ground. I wondered if he might kill me just for having heard all this. He was almost completely out of control, almost. But in a couple more minutes, the hostility cooled down to a grumble and Ray talked himself back to his priority, finding Jimmy. If it hadn't been obvious to me before, it was clear now: some of these guys were capable of anything.

This meeting was the last time I saw Little Ray Thompson, and the last words he spoke to me were curses. I never saw him again, dead or alive.

Three days before Ray killed him, Jimmy Savoy was stupidly hanging out at a local place called the Cricket Club—he might as well have driven around Fort Lauderdale with a bullhorn. Maybe he'd given up? Maybe he was hoping for forgiveness? Whatever it was, I'm pretty sure what happened was not what he expected. It wasn't long before Ray and four others swung by for a visit. Everything after that would be easy. Also bloody.

Here's what happened next, according to what came out in court. I'm not sure it's completely accurate, especially the role of my friend, Scott Errico, but this is what the court decided was true. Scott, Pat Menillo, and perhaps a few others captured Jimmy, bound his hands and feet with duct tape, and took him to a house where, as the court record delicately puts it, the men "questioned him" about the money in the safe and where the hell he'd been for the last six months. Torture continued for most of a day and night. The next morning, Ray and a small crew put Jimmy on a thirty-foot Scarab racing boat and continued the torture there. Waves were up to eight feet; the recommendation was for small boats not to go out. This one went anyway; by at least one account, Ray was already coked out of his mind, directing one of his men to blast Jimmy with his own billy club at every denial of guilt.

As for how it played out from there, all we have are untrustworthy witnesses who either carried out the crime or watched it go down.

Who knows exactly what happened or was said. All that's reasonably certain is that one or two men wrapped Jimmy in chains attached to an anchor, a total of about 150 pounds, about the same as what Jimmy weighed. Then Ray, high on coke and in a blind rage, blasted his old friend in the head with a .38 hollowpoint. The men pushed the headless body off the side and watched the weight carry it out of sight toward the bottom.

I didn't know it, but the Savoy murder was taking place around the same time my own trial was getting underway on March 23.

Chapter 16

DEFENDANT

The judge for my trial would be Stan Kaplan, a man the court-house crowd called "the hanging judge." He was tough, but not for the reasons you may think. He believed that enforcing the law as it was written was more important than reaching the desired outcome for any particular case or defendant. As I'll show you, that's the opposite of how a lot of people felt then and feel today. Judge Kaplan had been paralyzed from polio since age fourteen. He contracted it a year before the vaccine was ready. When I met him, he had spent almost three times as many years in a wheelchair than out of it. But he wasn't bitter. Just the opposite. I think he appreciated things more because he'd had to work so hard to get them. People who met him usually admired him. Today, his son is a judge on the same court his father served. I learned a lot just being around Stan Kaplan, both being a defendant in front of him and, eventually, receiving a sentence from him.

One fact was indisputable: I had been behind the wheel of a van full of pot. Our straightforward defense was that the stop had been illegal. If we could prove that, then the evidence gathered in the stop, 1,500 pounds of marijuana, was inadmissible. If any judge could set aside the pressure of the rising "Just Say No" culture and cut through to the law, it would be Judge Kaplan—we hoped.

I'd been pulled over without probable cause. No broken taillight, no rolling through a stop sign, no expired tags. You might think that cops are too smart to stop somebody without an obvious reason. Generally, they are. That's why these cops said they pulled me over on the basis of a tip. They said the tipster worked in Ray's boathouse and had provided the schedule for this particular van, as if random pot runs were scheduled like trains. Fortunately, he had called just in time with exactly the information they needed at exactly the right point in the investigation. Who says miracles don't happen? This fellow had casually betrayed his boss, the biggest gangster in Florida, to expose the biggest marijuana smuggling operation in American history.

I'll let you in on a little secret: there was no tipster. If they'd really had this information, and had it from a reliable source, they would have raced to the boathouse as soon as they heard it. But that's not what they did. They looked for a van coming out of the boathouse and hoped it would have pot in it, which would justify a raid on the warehouse the van came from. To do this inside the law, all they had to do was wait for some trivial violation to justify the stop, something as simple as doing 36 in a 35, but that's not what they did. Instead, they tried to be clever, and they manufactured this horseshit, probably out of a mix of ambition and pressure from headline-hungry Feds.

By the time the case got to court, the prosecution had realized how much baloney they'd have to slice in order to sell their tale of the phantom tipster, so they concocted a new story. Now they said that when the van came out of the boatyard, the bumper was dragging the ground. That, they said, meant it was loaded. Such a case would be open and shut.

"That's what the officer saw?" said Judge Kaplan.

"Yes, Your Honor," said the prosecutor.

"And that was the pretext for the stop?"

"Yes, Your Honor."

"Not for a brake light, nothing like that."

"No, Your Honor."

"You stopped a van coming out of a known stash house because the officer observed it was obviously loaded up."

"Yes, sir," said the prosecutor.

Now it was our turn. Dohn picked up a folder and handed it to the judge. Inside were two photos. One was the van, doors open, and empty. The other was the van, doors open, loaded up with 1,500 pounds of free weights, the same poundage as the pot they'd pulled at the stop—and the bumper wasn't dragging. In both photos, in fact, the bumper was within a quarter inch of the same height off the street.

"We took these last weekend," said Dohn. We'd requisitioned the van from impound, driven it to my friend's gym, and loaded it with free weights. Then we set up a ruler and took before-and-after shots.

"The officer told you he observed this bumper," Dohn said, "and that officer told you it was dragging. But as you can see, Judge Kaplan, the bumper wasn't dragging at all." It was as simple as that.

The judge granted our motion to suppress the evidence and the prosecution's case collapsed. Judge Kaplan didn't like ruling in my favor, but what he disliked even more was a prosecutor flouting the law to get a conviction. An investigation that had been underway for years was knocked out because the guys who were running it started cutting corners when they didn't have to. The result? I won. And now I was free.

But not really.

Chapter 17

WINNER

The risk to me was over for now, but the storm of the experience had tossed the pieces of my life all over the place.

Immediately after my arrest and getting out on bail, I holed up in my house for a week. I didn't even look in the mirror. I'd let everybody down. I was a first-rank fighter, headed for the championship. I had come face-to-face with a dubious opportunity and chosen wrong.

That careless, ridiculous quote I had given to the paper—you know, that I live like a drug smuggler but that I'm not really a drug smuggler? That idiot remark got attached to me like a ball and chain. For a while reporters hung out in front of my house. It was awful. I'm a guy who likes to see his name in the papers, but not like this. The *Miami Herald.* The Hollywood *Sun-Sentinel.* It seemed like my bad news was everywhere. I wouldn't have been surprised to pick up a grocery flier and find a paragraph about me next to the sale on broccoli.

My reputation as a squeaky-clean athlete? Gone. So were the benefits of being a rising star. Let's pick just one out of the big bag of regrets: Chuck Norris—*the* Chuck Norris, the champion martial artist, maybe the biggest ever, the creator of his own martial arts discipline, then a full-fledged action star in the movies—had become a friend. He had refereed my first professional fight and had liked me so much that he had given me a contract to appear in his next movie. I would have scored a big check, to say nothing of how it would have opened the door to all kinds of opportunities in Hollywood. But with the arrest, so much for that. And the other offers from movie studios that had been right in front of me? Gone, gone, gone.

The media had trashed me. It was my fault. I'd handed them all they needed to do it. In the legal system, though, I had not been convicted of anything at all. After a while, I realized that this was more important than what the papers said. It meant I was still free to try anything I wanted, free to make an appeal to the fans and the kickboxing associations, free to take fights, free to make my own reputation.

I had told Tonita that if I won the case, I'd marry her. When I won, she still wanted me, and I kept my promise. To celebrate, I threw a big party. Everyone came—that was a promising sign. And I began the slog back.

I was already a fighter in the ring. Now I would be a fighter in the press for my own good name. These were the days before the internet and thus before such a thing as an internet mob. People read the sports pages, watched the fights, had real conversations with people they knew from work and church and the bar. Folks made up their own minds about things, and they didn't rely on Facebook or Twitter to tell them what they ought to believe.

My press got better—not perfect, but better. A lot of it was this kind of thing: *He has money, he's famous in the martial arts world, he got off because the fix was in.* They even said the cops rigged the trial for one of their own, me, their self-defense trainer. Ha! If they only knew. Beyond that, the good stories started coming more often. I was taking serious fights and winning them. Sportswriters started following me and writing positive things, like the fact that I was good on both offense and defense. I'd been taking punches for too long. Now I was fighting back, and I was winning again.

As I was working toward the title, I got my first movie role. It was in an independent martial arts picture called *New York Chinatown.* I got to play the bad guy, and I had a blast working with one of the greatest kickboxers of all time, my friend Don "The Dragon" Wilson. It was his first movie, too.

He and I were having a big time playing at the movie business in Manhattan, but we both had big title fights coming up, so we needed to stay on our training schedules. One afternoon we decided to combine hanging out with working out by taking a run through Central Park. It's two and a half miles end to end, 59th to 110th, from just above Carnegie Hall to Harlem. We made it a five-mile run. By the end we decided the two champs had earned a nap, so we found a grassy spot in the park and laid down.

We forgot where we were: New York City in 1981, when the city was as crime ridden as it had been since they started keeping records. We also forgot that our fanny packs, the usual carry bags in those days, would look like an easy mark for a mugger. But we weren't worried.

We figured that two martial arts champs would intimidate anybody who tried to take us on. What we didn't figure is that we didn't look so intimidating when we were asleep. While we were napping, some jackass took our bags, including our money.

Don went to a pay phone to call his brother, Jimmy, who was also our manager. He had just one question for us: How in the heck did you two champs get robbed? Of course he didn't ask until after he stopped laughing. It ended up as a story and a cartoon panel in *Karate Today* magazine written by Jimmy himself. We were on the cover, though the headline was about our title fights, not our New York adventure. It was a brilliant public relations move by Jimmy. People inside the martial arts world told and retold the story for months.

A short six months after my appearance in front of Judge Kaplan, I had worked my way to a shot at the title. It was November 10, 1982, a twelve-round bout in Las Vegas. I was up against Steve Mackey, a great fighter out of Kansas City and the world champion. But to become the champion myself, I'd have to take it from him.

There was also a big TV piece about me on a show that was very popular at the time, *PM Magazine*. The hook was that I was starting to generate interest as an action star for the movies. To get a little experience and exposure, I'd been doing some modeling, mostly TV commercials and print work, and I'd made it to the cover of a few martial arts magazines like *Karate Today*. Now I was on the cusp of the world title, and this TV segment put it all together: karate, movies, and me. The host led off with this: "What would you think about a model who makes his living getting black eyes and swollen lips?"

"I'm not really gorgeous and I'm not really ugly," I said. "Whatever looks I have, I try to keep 'em." It got a laugh.

The week before, a Japanese film producer had come to court me and to watch the fight. He'd already booked my friend Don for another movie. Now he was counting on my winning the Mackey fight so he could market the picture starring two world champions. That made the TV show, too. "Ted looks like Chuck Norris a little bit," he said. I was all for it. If film companies over there were willing to bet on me, maybe Hollywood would see that and do the same.

To take the title from the current champion, it's an unwritten rule that you have to do it by knockout. It's rare that you walk away with the belt unless you put the champ on his back. This night there would be no knockout.

When the last bell rang and Steve was still standing, I was crushed. *That's it,* I thought. *I fought a good fight but not good enough.* This one would go to the judges. I waited for the decision, looking confident, but it was just a show. Everybody knew how this one would go, because the champ doesn't go down unless he literally goes down. Finally, the referee stepped between us at center ring while the announcer read the scores. The first judge gave it to Steve. The second judge gave it to me. Then came the last card call.

"The winner by decision . . . and the *new* super-middleweight kickboxing champion of the world, Ted Pryor!"

The place exploded. My friends poured into the ring. They crowded around and lifted me into the air. My brother grabbed the belt and ran around holding it over his head. I laughed at him and shouted over the noise, "I did all the work! How are you the one with the belt?"

The reporters closed in with the microphones and cameras, but I ignored their questions until I could first say what was on my heart, what I needed to say. I dedicated my win to my father, my sisters, and my brother, but most of all to the one who wasn't there. "My mother died only a few years ago," I said. "Right before she passed, she told me one thing, be sure and win that world title. So I dedicate this to my mom." The crowd exploded again. That night there were no tears, just the joy of victory. We hugged and shouted with the roaring Vegas crowd. I would hold my title from 1982 until 1987. That spectacular evening where it began remains the highlight of my life.

Now I would be fighting all over the world. In the many countries where martial arts are the American equivalent of football and baseball—Hong Kong, Japan, Thailand—I was welcomed as a celebrity, treated the way a famous quarterback would be treated in America. I rarely ate a meal where somebody didn't grab the check before I could. They wanted bragging rights, buying dinner for the champ. And I was getting good press, tons of it.

I defended my title four times: three KOs and one decision. One of my favorite title defenses—one of my favorite fights, period—was part of a five-fight event in West Palm Beach. Kickboxing champ Steve Shepherd put it together as a major event, which it was: US champion kickboxers in five weight classes against the best from the Soviet Union. It was a packed house, the excitement was as intense as I can remember at any bout, and our guys won every match.

There was a moment at the top of my fight that ratcheted up the tension a little more, although that was the last thing I intended. The Russians had a little ceremony—more of a tradition, really—at the start of each fight. When the bell rings, you come to the center of the ring and the Soviet fighter hands you a small Russian doll as a gesture of goodwill. Nobody told me this was coming, and I hadn't seen the other fights, so when I got in the ring, here was this guy I'd never met handing me a doll. I thought it was an insult. If he had been an American fighter, bet your ass the only reason he would do such a thing would be to start something. So, I took the doll and tossed it over my shoulder. A couple minutes later I knocked the guy out.

By the way, I wasn't pissed. There's no place for emotion in the ring. The smart play, the only play, is to treat fighting like a job. I never disliked an opponent, never wanted to hurt anybody. I just wanted to win the fight as quickly and as efficiently as possible. There's nothing like an elegant victory. Most of the guys I fought, we'd go out to dinner afterward and talk about how the fight went. We'd unwind, laugh, and encourage each other like professionals in any business. Then we'd talk about when and where we might fight again.

Also, these dinners were always, always after I'd won, and not because I was a sore loser who didn't go out when he lost. These dinners were always after a victory because I never lost. After going 0–5 from the start, I fought sixty-five times and took home sixty-five victories. No ties, no losses. All wins.

I loved being in the ring, still do. I know you think it hurts to take a punch, but lemme set you straight. To a conditioned fighter, a punch isn't painful. It's just a signal that tells you where your opponent is focused versus where he is not. In that way, it's a map that tells you where to hit him next. But that doesn't mean a punch can't put you down.

I was in Hong Kong with Joe Hess defending my title. I was in my room in the back, warming up, getting a little sweat going, when there was this noise on the other side of the wall, slow and steady. *Bang. Bang. Bang.* I asked Joe to check it out.

"It's the guy you're gonna fight," he said. "He's taped up his shins and he's slamming them against the wall."

"What the fuck? Lemme see."

Joe waved me off. "Let it go. But don't let this guy hit you in the leg, okay? 'Cos that's what this is about."

Joe was right. This guy was doing *tameshiwari*, the martial art of breaking things. Judging from the thick, old callus down his shin, it was the only tool he had, and when the bell rang for round one, he got right down to doing it. Over the course of the fight he hit me about a hundred times on my left leg, just above my knee, over and over, using that taped-up shin like an ax. My leg was a tree and he was going to chop at it until it fell.

Since I couldn't stop kicks like that, I had to deal with the result. He was bursting vessels in my leg, so if I sat down, it would swell up immediately and I wouldn't be able to stand again. That led me to an obvious strategy: I'd stand for the rest of the fight, no sitting between rounds. And while he was trying to burst the vessels in my thigh, I'd pummel him, hopefully wearing him down to the point that I could put him away.

We went at it like this for six rounds. Seconds into the seventh, I knocked him out. Good thing, because my leg wouldn't have held up much longer. While he went to the canvas, I went to the hospital, where they put my leg in an ice bucket for twenty-four hours. It was as painful as it sounds, more painful than the kicks.

Chapter 18

SCHEMER

I was a world champion kickboxer, but I was still a smuggler, too. I was always looking out for myself, and sometimes I had to look out for my partners, too—the business with Scott in Jamaica, for instance. Now it was Patrick's turn in the barrel.

In 1982, my partner and friend Patrick Bilton got arrested. Patrick had been up to his elbows in the Miami marijuana game since he was in his teens. He was twenty-seven, already an old hand at making runs across the Caribbean, and a master at staying off the radar, figuratively and literally, of the Florida Marine Patrol. He had a proven system that I remember because it involved a little trick I liked to do myself. He'd head out for the marijuana pickup with a pretty girl on board his boat, and he'd make sure everybody saw her. That way the drug run would look like a date.

A couple weeks after I won the championship, Patrick headed out on his thirty-footer, *Midnight Express*. He was with a girl named Patti Hunwick, a real-life Playboy Bunny and the wife of Bernard "Barry the Bear" Hunwick, who was fresh off an acquittal for running a nationwide squad of hit men. Never mind the pot smuggling. When your first mate is a Playboy Bunny married to an accused and later convicted hit man, you're living dangerously—not that Patrick knew Barry's business. All he saw was a pretty girl on his bow. When Patrick found out about the connection between his female first mate and Barry—and what Barry did—he shit himself. Literally, if memory serves.

Patrick made his package pickup and turned back for Florida, but this was one of those days that the patrol got suspicious. Maybe they just wanted to meet a Playboy Bunny. Who knows? Whatever the reason, they came after him. With a quarter ton of marijuana on board, this was one stop he couldn't let happen, so he took off across the Intracoastal. If he could get into international waters, he'd be out of their jurisdiction, where he could float around or even press on to Bimini until things cooled off.

The Marine Patrol boat pushed so hard that their engines blew. That should have been the end of it, except the agents switched tactics. Moments before Patrick was about to cross into international waters, a police helicopter came overhead and ordered him to cut his engines. He was too close to stop now. Having upgraded from a boat to a chopper, the agents overhead also upgraded from loudspeakers to firearms. They blasted all four of Patrick's engines. His boat was dead in the water. Patrick wondered if he was, too.

Like the five hundred pounds of pot, the case was also cut and dried, so, as usual, the trial wasn't nearly as big a moment as the sentencing. To make it worse, all this happened while Patrick was on probation. Put that in the big bowl of justice and stir it around? He was facing up to thirty years.

If there's one thing that I and all the guys in this story have in common, it's that the odds don't matter to us. We don't give up. Patrick was gonna take thirty years? Like hell he was.

One of our occasional partners was a guy named Dennis McGuire. Dennis had a legitimate business as a developer, so when our smuggling operations hit trouble, his above-board connections could often part the clouds. He would be Patrick's key to beating the sentence, and it involved a truly crazy scheme. With that in mind, follow me:

Dennis was friends with Elton J. Gissendanner—what a name, right? (He was a veterinarian who boasted that he could spay or neuter any dog in under three minutes. Really. Just to make this weirder.)

Elton was the head of the Florida Department of Natural Resources, known as the DNR. This was the organization in charge of the Florida Marine Patrol, and it was the Florida Marine Patrol that had arrested Patrick.

Do you see where this is going? With one phone call to Dennis, Patrick was about one bribe away from crawling out from under thirty years in the old graybar hotel. Of course he had the money and Dennis was happy to help—he and Patrick had been smuggling buddies for ages, which meant they both had big things at stake. This left one question: Would Elton, the head of the DNR, take the bribe?

C'mon, man. He was hanging out with the guys on our team. What do you think?

They came up with a plan: Patrick would give Dennis $100K to pass along to Elton. In exchange, Elton would press the agents to go easy on Patrick. He even threw in a bonus: he would personally press the judge for a lighter sentence. To make it all seem legit, there was one more condition, and it was a big one: Patrick had to become a confidential informant. It was the only way to excuse Elton going easy on a smuggler when this kind of case was the state's biggest priority.

But here's the twist: none of us intended for Patrick to become a confidential informant. Instead, we'd offer up an elaborate put-on so it only looked that way.

I should know. I helped him do it.

Long before all this, Patrick and Scott bought a forty-five-foot Hatteras. They invited me to put in fifty grand to be a part owner, and I did. We named it the *Tunita*. (Close to my wife's name, but not quite. We chose that as an inside joke, another dumb move that waved like a red flag to later connect me to the smuggling operation.) They'd do the smuggling and pay me as a silent partner.

Weird fact: if you watch reruns of *Miami Vice*, you've seen the boat. It was featured in the pilot episode. In the story, they filled it with pot—not real pot, I'm sure, but you never know—so the stars of the show, Don Johnson and Philip Michael Thomas as Detectives Sonny Crockett and Rico Tubbs, could do a bust on the *Tunita* as it pulled up at the pier. I saw it on TV myself, though I hadn't known Patrick and Scott had rented it out for the show. Talk about a surprise. You don't expect to see your own property on a popular TV show, let alone being put to the illegal use it was bought for in the first place. But that's what I saw. Art imitates life, right?

All of that matters because to get Patrick out of this tight spot, we were required to sacrifice a boat. Since we all owned a piece of the *Tunita,* we went with that one.

This was the plan. First, we'd load up the boat with three kilos— three "keys" of coke. By the way, when I say "load up," that's an over-statement, because three keys don't take up much room. A key is about the size of a piece of Texas toast. So when I say "loaded up," we weren't backing up a truck. You can carry three keys in your coat pocket.

But here's the thing: we'd tell Patrick that there would be fifty keys on the boat, worth about a million and a quarter in cash. With Patrick not knowing it was only three, he'd be more believable when he did his informant routine.

How could Patrick promise fifty keys and get away with the cops finding only three? We'd run the boat aground in the corals about three miles short of the destination, rip the three keys open to look like they were left behind in a hurry, then we'd bail on a raft. The cops would see the coke as the remnants of getting out in a hurry.

Three keys, a bribe, and a used boat: all totaled, it was about $375,000 out of our pockets, and more than a fair price to beat a thirty-year sentence. Plus the take would be enough to satisfy the cops and give them a good headline, which was always high on their list of priorities.

The night of the deal arrived. We ditched on the coral, broke open the keys, spread the loose coke around the deck, then bailed in the dinghy. Keep in mind that Patrick didn't know the details. All he knew was to promise fifty keys at a certain time and place. And at that promised time and place, with the cops waiting beside him, Patrick and his promise fell through. That's what we wanted him to think so when it went down with the agents watching, it would seem real to them because it was real to him.

He didn't have to suffer for long. Minutes later an agent found our subterfuge, the *Tunita* aground on the coral, seemingly by accident but just like we planned.

The promised payoffs fell neat like dominoes. Bribe in hand, Elton pushed the agents to go easy on Patrick, and with Patrick's "delivery" of the *Tunita* he didn't have to push too hard. For the cherry on top, Elton even wrote that letter to the sentencing judge, as promised, and on state stationery. He called for leniency for a fine young man who had turned from the smuggling game to help the intrepid representatives of law enforcement take off the table a cache of drugs and a drug-smuggling vessel worth $200,000. The judge gave Patrick parole.

The receipt: one aging boat, three keys of coke, a hundred grand in bribes (seems it was $80K for Elton and $20K for Dennis, though who can say for certain?), and a few hours of adventure worthy of an action movie. The money we spent could be made up in a single smuggling run, yet it bought Patrick's freedom and our ability to keep doing all this. As the old MasterCard commercial used to go, *priceless*.

Chapter 19

LITIGANT

On the day in front of Judge Kaplan that gave me back my life, there was one loose end. The charges had been set aside, not dismissed, meaning they could be brought back at any time. While I was traveling the world as the kickboxing champ, prosecutors spent their time looking for a way to drag me back in, another tool to pressure the other players.

Their primary goal was to get the appeals court to overrule Kaplan about the illegal stop. If they could do that, they could drag me out of my wonderful life—in the middle of a fight, if they wanted to be dramatic—cuff me, and put me on trial as if the first time never happened.

If I'm making it sound like I was the center of the storm, believe me, I wasn't. Remember, this was all about getting Little Ray. He owned the boatyard, he ran the operation, and he was the kingpin.

I mattered because I could be useful in getting to him. I'd spent two years clawing my way out of the hole I'd dug—make no mistake, I made the choice and brought this on myself; I don't blame anybody else. I was close to having my life back under my control. But the Feds had never stopped coming after me, and, as the possibility appeared that the reversal they needed might happen, they decided to let me know I was in their sights.

I would walk out to my car, glance at the bumper and have the feeling that something wasn't right. Sure enough, I'd reach under and find a bug—a tiny radio broadcasting my location and perhaps even my voice. I found several, sometimes inside the car, sometimes on it or under it, but always poorly hidden, like they wanted me to find it. Because they did.

Any other time in my life I might have gotten worked up about it, but in those days I did not. I had beaten the rap, and they were as steamed at that as they were about not being able to nab Ray. It made sense that they would bug me, or at least leave bugs to try to upset me. They were hoping to knock me off balance, catch me at something questionable or illegal. But I wasn't going to let that happen.

My lawyer, Dohn Williams, knew all this was going on but decided the best thing for my peace of mind and my martial arts career was to keep it from me. If something big came up, he'd call. In 1984, he did.

He gave it to me straight, but, since I'd spent the last two years being treated like a king, I had trouble realizing that anything was bad news. He decided to deliver the new information not in his office but over a Saturday night dinner in a fancy restaurant, maybe so I'd take it a little more calmly.

"What do you mean, it's back on?" I said. "Judge Kaplan tossed the charges. The cops have been harassing me but that's nothing new. I'm a world champion. I'm on the straight and narrow. They got nothing."

"Ted, none of that matters," he said. "They just won their appeal."

Judge Kaplan had ruled that they pulled me over without probable cause, which made the 1,500 pounds of pot inadmissible as evidence. Without the evidence, they had no case. Now the prosecutors had taken the case to a higher court, claiming that Judge Kaplan was wrong, and that's just the ruling they got.

The way I see it, the Feds were putting pressure on Florida because the whole "Just Say No" thing was in full swing, and the Amity bust was the biggest bust to date in US history. The appeals ruling came from Judge Hugh Glickstein, a man with a long history of doing good things for the community, especially advocating for the rights of children. But Judge Glickstein had also evolved into a guy who believed the ends justified the means. In my case, the cops said a mysterious "concerned citizen" (I'm quoting from Glickstein's decision) had called, insisted on staying anonymous, and told the agents that the warehouse was full of marijuana. Judge Glickstein said that was all they needed. He called it "common sense." I believe the cops concocted a phantom informer to justify their hunch and, when they realized it wouldn't stand up in court, they lied about the dragging bumper. The appeals judge said they need not have bothered with the bumper story. The bullshit from their phantom would do just fine.

The next time you get pulled over in Florida on nothing more than a cop's hunch, you can thank the late Judge Glickstein, whose interest in the law ended where his priorities for society began, with a little pressure from the Feds to help him make up his mind. Since the law didn't give prosecutors the outcome they wanted, he decided the law meant something else.

You may be reading this and saying that since I was smuggling pot, it's great that a judge shrugged off some technicality to convict me. I understand why you'd feel that way. Here's my side. People say "technicality" like they're spitting out poison because it means that one part of the law is getting in the way of enforcing some other part. But if it's okay to ignore some part of the law sometimes, which laws and when? Imagine courts where the judge isn't bound by the law. A judge could do whatever he likes. That's what Glickstein did to me. Upholding the Constitution should protect people who are falsely accused, as well as people who are guilty.

As for the law I was breaking, some rights shouldn't be subject to majority rule. If three guys get together and two of them vote to beat the shit out of the other, that's majority rule, but it's no way to live. Some rights are, as the Declaration of Independence says, inalienable. One is that it's wrong to tell people what they can and cannot put in their bodies. You don't have to use pot—I don't and never have—to agree that it's wrong to deny people a choice, even when it's not the choice you'd make. People wanted what we sold, and if anybody got hurt, it wasn't because pot killed them. It was because of the pot business, which was deadly only because it was illegal.

I was back where I had been two years before. The prosecution would get another shot. If they had to drown me to get to Ray, they were happy to do it. This led to another big change. "I can't stay on as your lawyer," said Dohn. "My firm represents Ray. That's a conflict. I have to step back."

The ethics rules for lawyers may have led to this conclusion, but the reality of things mattered most. Ray was in a world of trouble, Ray was still the boss, and he needed not only Dohn's undivided attention but also his undivided loyalty. Ray wasn't about to risk letting Dohn juggle my interests against his own, and Dohn sure as hell didn't want to. One mistake and his career would come to a quick end under a front-page Florida headline, "Promising Local Attorney Found Shot to Death." It was true that he was ethically bound to resign my case. It was also true that the only way for Dohn to keep himself literally and figuratively above ground was to pass me along to someone else.

He gave me some parting advice, wise stuff as usual. "You gotta cooperate," he said. "You don't do that, you're gonna spend five to fifteen years in prison." He said the best guy to make my deal would be Jon Sale. "He's one of the most highly respected lawyers I know and he has a great reputation with the judges and prosecutors," said Dohn. "They all trust him."

Now that Dohn had sent me in a new direction, I needed a strategy for what was next. I got it from someone I won't name here: "You go in there and you don't have to remember everything. Pick somebody inside Ray's organization, somebody you don't like. Tell the investigators everything you know but instead of mentioning Ray, use the name of that other guy. You roll on Ray," this person said, "he'll kill you." This was coming from someone in a position to know. I knew it was true. Still, it was a hell of a thing to hear.

I knew what I needed to do: take my time spinning out the story, five or six hours, maybe more. This was important because there needed to be a record of a cordial conversation. I needed whoever interviewed me to say I cooperated freely and to not challenge my truthfulness. That way, if they figured out the real story, the judge would focus on them, not me. He'd want to know why they didn't question my honesty in the first place.

As I reflected on my situation, the gravity of it settled in. I reminded myself that I was returning to face Judge Kaplan. His resentment simmered from being overruled, and those prosecutors had dared to challenge his authority. Their actions had consequences for both of us. Cooperation became my only recourse: by demonstrating cooperation, I gave the judge the latitude to exercise his discretion and potentially spare me from the mandatory sentence. That was the hope—the way out I needed.

Who knew? Maybe it would work. The state would finally get what they wanted in the first place, a paved pathway to nailing Little Ray Thompson. And that path ran right through me.

Chapter 20

CULPRIT

They arrested me. I didn't put up a fight. Why bother? One more time with the intake, one more time with the booking and the fingerprinting and the lockup. And when it came time for the interrogation, I followed the script.

They put me in a room with a pair of very angry cops. These two gave me the whole punk-ass routine, slamming their hands on the table and yelling and threatening—which I suppose gave them an extra thrill, because how often can you disrespect a world-champion kickboxer to his face and leave the room without a broken arm? I wanted to give them what their attitude was begging for. It was only my athlete's self-discipline that kept me from cracking their heads together and adding that to the indictment. They could afford their anger. I couldn't. Besides, I understood their anger. They felt betrayed because I'd been one of them. Now I wasn't.

Over the course of about six hours, I told them my story. I replaced Ray Thompson with someone else, Pat Menillo. In my opinion he was the slimiest gangster in the outfit, a quiet guy prone to explosions of violence. When you looked in his eyes you saw nothing but anger, nothing but hollowness. I figured Pat would kill anybody who looked at him sideways, kill them in a New York minute. He'd make a good proxy for Ray. So I told the cops what I knew about Ray, but I said it was Pat.

Jon A. Sale was a serious man still early in his career, but it had already been a major one. A decade before, he had been an assistant prosecutor in the Watergate affair, one of the guys who felt the fallout of the famous "Saturday Night Massacre," when Nixon ordered the attorney general to fire Special Prosecutor Archibald Cox. One year later, Nixon was gone. Jon was there for it all. Years later, Jon represented Mayor Rudy Giuliani during the Trump years, and he was offered and turned down the opportunity to represent President Trump himself. In 1984 he was representing me. He dealt with white-collar crime, not drug stuff, but for this case he made an exception. I'm lucky he did.

Jon assured me we had an advantage because Judge Kaplan was a fair judge. I was glad for that, but I had a history with the judge, too, and he liked me as well. Despite the rough company I had kept, the company that had put me in front of him, it seemed to me he sensed that there was something better in me, something that ought not be extinguished before it could lead me to something better.

Still, Jon was an attorney, not a magician. The case had been pretty clear the first time. Now, with the previously inadmissible evidence in play, there wasn't much he could do to get me out of this. The court found me guilty. Now Judge Kaplan would hand down my sentence.

The first time I faced him, the prosecution's overreach had saved me. Now that they'd gotten away with it, all I could rely on was Judge Kaplan's opinion of me as a person to temper the punishment. I knew what mattered most to him was the law, which is as it should be. Still, I hoped he might factor in what he thought about me. I also figured he was angry over the ends-justify-the-means way this case had come back to him.

The judge told us that he had to sentence me according to the law. No surprise there. Jon answered that because of my cooperation, I deserved a lighter sentence. That set off the prosecution like a fire alarm.

"But he didn't cooperate!" they said. They told Judge Kaplan that everything I had given them had been lies—at the very least, the name had been wrong. They were correct. And this is where the strategy from my anonymous advisor paid off: *They're gonna have a hard time painting you as an uncooperative witness if you actually cooperate.*

"Show me the transcripts," said Judge Kaplan. These transcripts amounted to a stack nearly four feet tall—over six hours of conversation. "You mean to tell me you guys sat here for most of a day and you didn't get one true word out of this man's mouth?" he said.

"That's absolutely right," said the prosecutor. He said I lied. He said I blamed other people. He said I gave them the wrong name. "And we knew the real name the whole time," he said.

With that answer, the trap was sprung.

"Hold on," said the judge. "If you knew the name, why did you let Mr. Pryor sit there for six hours and tell you a story you knew was a lie?"

Bingo! "If he didn't cooperate," continued Kaplan, "you would have shut that thing down thirty seconds after he started lying to you." He turned to me. "Mr. Pryor, how many times did they interrupt you to say you were lying?"

"None," I said, and it was the truth.

"Mr. Pryor was in fact a cooperative witness. That matters," he said, before turning his frustration on the prosecution. He told them he was tired of all the false stories on top of false stories. "Nobody sits there listening to lies all day if they aren't getting something out of it." That was the end of the discussion. The prosecution's role was over. No more debate. Now it was all up to Judge Kaplan, who would hand down my sentence.

"Mr. Pryor, I'm going to have to send you away. I don't want to give you a long sentence, but I have to adhere to the law," he said. I assume he was thinking of the failure of the appeals court to do the same. "Therefore, I am under certain constraints. The least amount of time I can give you is one year in county jail."

That was tough, but it would be something I could take. Except now Jon threw a curve into the whole thing. "Your Honor," he said, "instead of county jail for a year, would you consider sentencing my client to a longer sentence in one of Florida's penitentiaries?"

Read that again, friends: my lawyer just asked the judge if he could move me from county lockup to state pen and increase my sentence. I figured Jon had had a stroke or something. I was about to have one myself.

"Your Honor, may I please have a moment with my attorney? Because it doesn't sound like Jon can do math."

"No, no," Jon said. "We don't need a minute. If you'll move him to the state institution, he'll take the longer term with it."

"No, he won't," I said. "Your Honor, may we have a moment?" And boy, did I take that moment. Before I could ask a question, he cut me off and, out of Kaplan's earshot, told me his plan. It's a peculiarity of Florida law that a sentence up to a year puts you in county lockup, but longer than that puts you in the penitentiary.

"The state pen is where you want to be," said Jon. "If you go to state prison you get a thing called gaintime. For every day you show good behavior, they knock one day off your sentence. So instead of, say, a year and a half in state pen, you do nine months—you cut your sentence in half. Besides, I can get you in a work release facility in three months anyway."

It sounded too good to be true, but if he was right, it made sense: take a longer sentence, keep your nose clean, and the system automatically trims the time back to something even the judge couldn't offer. Since Jon came to me through Dohn, I trusted him. We turned back to the judge. "Your Honor, my client is going to take the longer term in state," said Jon.

"Have you lost your mind?" said the judge. "Mr. Pryor, you were right the first time about arithmetic, but apparently you have something in mind. If this is what you want, that's what I'll give you."

When they sentence you to prison in state court, they take you away in handcuffs that very moment. Jon said he would try something creative and ask to follow the process used in federal court, where they allow voluntary surrender at a later date. Jon asked for sixty days for me to report to prison. Not only did Judge Kaplan go along with it, he gave me ninety days, citing my character and my comeback, especially how I'd been traveling the world as a kickboxing champion and conducting myself with honor. "Mr. Pryor has in this way redeemed himself," he said. He said he regretted sentencing me today because his original ruling two years before had been correct. He also said that he was aware that there might be those who wanted something other than justice under the law for this case. To me, that was a nice way of saying that there were agents and prosecutors involved not for justice but for notches on their belt in pursuit of a hotshot career.

Prison would also end my run as world champion. I had defended my title four times in four years, but I couldn't fight from prison. The rule was simple. When a year passes without a title defense, the association takes the title away, and that's what they did. I would attempt a comeback a few years later, but I'd feel it in my bones that those days had passed. I decided it was time to move on to the next challenge, to become as big a success in business as I had been as a kickboxer. I'm happy with that decision, but it's hard to walk away even when you know it's the smart play. There's something about being the champ that feels better than anything else you can name. Fighting, the thing that I loved the most and had been the center of my life, was over. But the need to be the champ at whatever you do? That feeling was still in me.

Chapter 21

PRISONER

I spent the ninety days tying up my affairs. That time went by in a second. On the day I was due to surrender, I rented a little prop plane with my brother Tony and my good friend George Monsoor. We landed at an airstrip near Lake Butler, home of the Reception and Medical Center, the prisoner intake facility. It's not far off Alligator Alley, where I had made my first smuggling run a few years before. With the plane, I figured that at least I'd arrive in style. When we landed, Tony pointed across the way.

"One more thing," he said. "How about this?"

A long, black limousine was waiting for the three of us. I looked at him, grinned, shrugged my shoulders. "What the hell?"

"Champ oughta arrive in style, dontcha think?" he said. "C'mon, bro. Get in."

Picture the contrast: on a muggy, greasy Florida afternoon, a spotless-shiny black limo pulls up in front of a prison—the dreariest, plainest shin-kick of a place you can imagine. Barbed wire. Watchtowers. Pissed-off, moonfaced guards with machine guns in their hands, the whole joint all concrete and grim. It occurred to me that nobody pulls up here and literally surrenders. If you were the least bit smart, you'd make them catch you all over again.

I said a few words to my brother and to George. The gist of it was my regret plus my usual commitment to grinding through whatever was next. *I gotta go, guys. Gotta do my time. Put this behind me. So I can get on with my life.*

Two nonspeaking guards escorted me through one set of gates, then another. The doors slammed behind me, seemingly slower and more deliberately and louder than they had to. I think that's on purpose: the guys who run it want to underline the difference between the open air you're leaving and the hard way ahead. Not five minutes later I heard my earlier thought said out loud. "Boy, you're checking yourself in?" said a guard, the first one to speak to me. "You must be one stupid cracker." He was right. That's how I felt, like one stupid cracker.

Turns out this was more than tough talk for the new guy. For the first time it occurred to me that this was not just a lousy place to be, it was genuinely dangerous. This was and remains the entry point for every prisoner in the state's charge. I wasn't in here just with check forgers and small-time hoods. This was a bad-guy stew. You want to see a murderer, a rapist, an armed robber, a child molester, a wife killer, an arsonist? Tap anybody on the shoulder and sooner or later you'll find one.

On arrival they grade you so they know where to put you. At the time there were five categories from cream puff to maniac. Since I could be as nice as a cream puff and as tough as a maniac, I wasn't sure how they'd classify me. I guess they didn't know, either, 'cos they went away and thought about it, and when they came back they put me right in the middle, medium security. I was relieved but I have to admit that I was a tiny bit disappointed that they didn't find me so intimidating that they tried to put me in hardcore lockdown. Not that I wanted it, but when you've just spent years flying around the world as a kickboxing champion, you get used to a certain level of respect in that area.

And respect was in short supply. Next up, haircut. The prisoner who was cutting hair—some wise fellow had put an electric metal tool in his hand; how smart was that?—asked me what kind of haircut I wanted. I had long hair at the time. I brushed it a bit with my fingers. "A little off the sides, please," I said, pleased that perhaps I had been wrong about this place! This dank Florida prison had seen fit to hire an aesthetician, and a friendly one at that. What else might they have, wine with dinner? An aperitif of the gentleman's choice? White tablecloths? Perhaps someone would come by with a hot towel for the champ before I retire for the evening?

BAWWWWWZZZZ! The prison barber, and I use that term very loosely since he was just a nut with a Norelco, shaved a two-inch stripe of bald down the middle of my head. He considered his work, then cackled like he'd heard his first joke. This was followed by the quickest, sloppiest haircut of all time, not counting every haircut he gave before or after. The style I had been assigned was slick bald, same as everyone else. Something about lice, they said. Whatever.

As Jon had arranged, I was soon transferred to work release.

Guess where they sent me: the very same work-release facility where I'd worked years before, the Pompano Correctional Office on Atlantic Avenue. It was like old times—well, except for which side of the desk I now occupied—right down to the company I would keep, because the chief of the place was now Barry Eringer, the guy I had started with. We both came in as CC-Ones. Now I was a guest, so to speak, and he was the man in charge. We'd kept in touch over the years. He knew me. He knew my wife. And now he would be in charge of me completely, in a situation where I was entirely vulnerable.

"Ted," he said, "what in the fuck did you do with your life? You're a fighter, a really good one. You train the cops. You're one of us."

"Yeah," I said.

"And look at where you are. You're a convict. This is your life now, Ted."

"Barry, I'm not in the mood for speeches. I know this better than anybody else—"

"I'm not sure you do," he said.

"I fucked up. Is that what you wanted to hear? I just want to get over my time."

"You fuck me, you're dead." He was in charge; I was the prisoner. How was I gonna fuck him over?

"I never fucked you over before," I said.

"That's a good start," he said. Then, with the obligatory warning out of the way, Barry tossed me a lifeline. He talked me through the generous details of what he called "privileges." I'd still be on work release, but I'd have latitude if I was willing to use it responsibly.

Now I understood why he had said not to fuck him on this. While the other guys would get dropped off in the morning and picked up in the afternoon by a van, I'd be allowed to come and go in my own car. I'd leave at nine in the morning and had to be back at five in the afternoon—not one minute after, but five o'clock on the nose if not before. He made it clear that what I did between nine and five wasn't that important. My real job was to stay out of trouble.

When I told Barry the truth, that I was disappointed in myself and wanted to turn things around, he believed me. For that he was willing to go out on a limb for me. Barry stood up for me, another case of friendship coming through.

I was pretty good about keeping Barry's rules—pretty good, not perfect. These days I've learned that some lines you don't cross. That makes for a far more satisfying and successful life. But back then I was proud, and I hadn't yet taken the lesson entirely to heart. Call it the hazards of believing you're indestructible.

About ninety days into my work release, I decided to bend the rules even further than Barry was already letting me. One Friday afternoon, I decided to catch a matinee with Tonita. That would have been nothing remarkable except that this was some kind of holiday—to this day I still don't know exactly which—and state employees had the day off. As Tonita and I emerged from the movies at the Broward Mall, I saw a familiar face. "Ted Pryor?" he said.

"Judge Kaplan, hi!" I shook his hand and held my breath.

"Ted," he said, "aren't you supposed to be doing time?"

"Yes, Your Honor. I served my sentence and now I'm on work release."

"What kind of work are you doing at the movies?"

I figured the smart move was to play it straight. "Truth is, I just took a couple hours with my wife to catch a matinee." It wasn't clear whether the hanging judge was good with that or if he was planning to use part of the rest of his day off to turn me in.

"Your lawyer's Jon Sale, right? Have him give me a call," he said, and he rolled away. I was relieved he didn't have me arrested on the spot, but who knew what the judge was going to do? If he pushed on this at all, not only would I end up in trouble, but Barry could be fired. I called Jon immediately, and he gave what I can only imagine was an Academy Award–worthy performance. He told the judge that I had made a terrible, stupid mistake. He explained that the blowback would affect Barry, who didn't deserve the trouble. He offered his personal assurance that nothing like this would happen again. All he asked in return was the biggest request he could make, that the judge not turn me in.

Judge Kaplan told Jon that he'd keep this one to himself. Why? I never asked. My first instinct is to remember it as the judge giving me yet another break, yet I know that wasn't his thinking. When things had gone my way in his courtroom, it was because the law had been on my side. The judge had been sympathetic to my situation when others had twisted the law against me. So maybe he saw this as an opportunity to right a bit of the wrong in all that. Who knows? Whatever his reasons, his decision kept me out of further trouble and kept Barry from ending up in a mess. I'll always be grateful.

It was the last squall before the next shitstorm, the biggest one of all.

Chapter 22

RUNNER

I t was another day in work release. Lesson learned, and now I was keeping my head down. Most of the time I'd spend the day with my wife at our townhouse, other times I had business, and when I did I made it quick. On this day I needed to meet with Dennis McGuire, the developer who'd gotten Patrick out of trouble.

We were meeting at a place called Crackers when I found out that things were about to go crazy. "I got good news and bad news," he said. I told him I'd take the bad news first. Boy, was it bad.

"You're on the front page of the *Miami* fucking *Herald*," he said.

And I was. Everything that had come before, everything I thought I'd either buried or gotten away with or was paying for right now? It was all back, all dragged out into the sunlight, the whole fucking mess that had seemed tucked away and fading out was alive again, spitting and racing to destroy all of whatever I'd managed to rebuild. This time, the attack, the retribution, the justice (if you want to call it that) was coming from more than the state and local guys. Suddenly all their shit seemed tame. This time, what was coming down would be backed by the full faith and credit of the federal government of the United States of America.

A half dozen DC law enforcement agencies had loaded this cannon. I was one of the gnats they'd aimed it at. About four dozen of us had been implicated or indicted in the federal version of the Ray Thompson investigation. The headline writers had finally figured out to go with the lede, that the boathouse bust years before was in fact the largest in American history.

Before cellphones and texts, the only way to contact somebody was by calling a landline. If you were away from a landline, the only other way to get you was through a beeper. The early ones didn't send any message. You just called a number, the beeper would go off, and it would display the number of who had called. That day, there with Dennis, my beeper went off. The only person who had the number was Barry. When he set me up with privileges, he'd given it to me as my leash. "I ever beep you," he said, "you'd better come. Don't get me fired." How did I still have the privileges that Barry and this beeper afforded? I'd never told him about the close call with Judge Kaplan. Now Barry was yanking the leash.

I wasn't 100 percent surprised by the blowup in the paper. I knew they were working on something. A few months earlier, the Feds had come to me with a deal: *Cooperate with us and we won't indict you. You can walk with state-time served. All you have to do is roll on the rest of the guys.* I should have taken the offer, but I didn't. What was I gonna tell them? I didn't roll on Ray in large part because I couldn't. I didn't know shit about the inner workings of Ray's operation.

I had dodged so many bullets already, surely I could dodge one more. Even when they managed to get a conviction against me, I had received a light sentence, then we'd transformed eighteen months behind bars into only three months, the rest as work release. I attributed my good fortune to the indestructible champ beating the odds one more time. In fact, I had come this far on good lawyering, lucky breaks, and law enforcement trying to stretch their thin evidence further than it would go.

As far as I could tell, they couldn't prove much of anything between Ray and me because there wasn't much I'd done. Where they ended up, a charge of conspiracy, had never occurred to me. The story in the paper had words like *multiple counts* and *organized crime* and, for the knockout, *fifty years to life*. "Scary" only begins to describe it.

Turns out I didn't understand something: what you and I think of as conspiracy isn't what the federal government means. They were talking RICO, the Racketeer Influenced and Corrupt Organizations Act of 1970. RICO makes the crimes of others "sticky." Even if you only have a tiny role, working on the fringes like me, the Feds can associate you with the crimes of the whole operation. Say you committed a robbery. You might go to jail for a few months or years and that's the end of it. But if you're also connected to some ongoing criminal enterprise, even slightly, they can slap you with a RICO charge related to whatever the bigger operation is up to. Suddenly your eighteen-month sentence turns into twenty years in federal prison. They can also confiscate everything you have. All that is what makes RICO so powerful: it gives the government profound leverage—the threat of decades in prison and complete bankruptcy—to make lower-level players flip on the higher-ups.

My beeper went off over and over. I silenced it each time, but Barry kept coming. I could hear him in my brain: *Don't fuck me, Ted. Don't you fucking fuck me.*

"Maybe you oughta catch that?" said Dennis.

"It's the guy who supervises me. I'm still on work release."

"You," said Dennis, "are fucking nuts."

The next time it went off, I found a pay phone and called Barry. "Where the fuck are you?" he said. "You get back here, Ted. Right now. Don't you fuck me!"

"Barry," I said, "calm down," which was the wrong thing for a guy in my position to say, especially to a guy in his position—and I didn't know just how bad his position was.

"Ted, I'm standing here in the middle of a bunch of federal officers, and these Feds are here for you. FBI, DEA, Secret Service, Treasury, you name it. Reporters are here, Ted. Everyone's looking for you, and they don't know where you are 'cos *I* don't know where you are."

"I'm coming," I said.

"All you have going for you is that they think you're at work, and I can't cover for you much longer. Get your ass back here. I'm on the chopping block with you."

It was one of the moments where the tension suddenly made me calm. "I'm coming back. Tell them that you just called me, which you did, and that I'm on my way."

"That's more like it."

"It'll be about four hours."

"The hell it will! Get here now."

"Barry, I'm gonna be fine. You're gonna be fine. I'm coming back. I just have a little accounting problem. I'll put that away and be right there."

"Accounting problem? You got a bigger problem—" but I hung up before he could finish his sentence. The accounting problem was the other half of why I was meeting with Dennis. We hadn't gotten past the bad news to the good news: he had delivered to me a suitcase with cash in it, my take from the latest runs.

"You want to count it?" he said, the sarcastic son of a bitch.

I laughed. "I'm gonna have to trust you today, Dennis. You never screwed me before," I said.

"Not yet," he said.

I grabbed the suitcase and took off. I was walking around with cash, and I had to stow it right then. At any moment the Feds could be all over me. First thing was hiding the money. Suddenly it came to me: *call a plumber.*

Before we go any further, know that I didn't mean it like a figure of speech, like plumber is a nickname for somebody with a particular criminal skill. I needed somebody who could get his hands on plenty of lengths of PVC pipe and, if I was lucky, solvent cement to glue them shut on both ends.

I called my brother—not a plumber, but the next best thing. He'd know where to get the pipes, then we'd stuff in the money, seal them shut, and bury them. That way if anybody happened to dig and find them, they'd figure it was water or sewage and leave it alone.

After we packed the pipes, I raced to the townhouse and buried them under the deck. I couldn't just give the cash to Tonita. Besides not wanting her in the line of fire, I knew that if I gave it to her, I'd never see it again. She was a shopaholic. I'd seen plenty of months where I'd sit down to pay bills, only to find she'd spent thousands on purses and shoes she'd never use. With the cash in the pipes, my nest egg was safe from cops, safe from being spent, safe from random dis-covery, and safe from any of the guys I knew who might come sniffing around.

With that done, I returned to face the music. Irony got piled on top of irony: I would be taken into custody while I was already in custody.

Chapter 23

COOPERATOR

ack at work release, state cops, local cops, federal agents, and reps from an alphabet soup of law enforcement agencies were amped up and ready. They were so excited to finally get their man that they seemed to forget all about having to wait for me. They handcuffed me, just like before, and tossed me in a van with some other men including Mike, Bobby Sheer, and Dwayne Durham, known as the Beach Boys, all from Ray's crew.

It was about an hour to Belle Glade, Florida, and Glades Correctional Institution, a nasty fuck of a prison, home of the hardcore. A decade later, a half dozen men, five of whom were murderers, would crawl out of the place through a tunnel eight feet deep and two feet wide, needing only seventy-five feet to get beyond the wall. Two decades after that, the state would shut it down. It really was a hellhole. It didn't have cells, just dormitories with stacked bunk beds, and no bathrooms, just open showers across from a line of commodes. It served as a warehouse for the worst guys, so much so that even the main guard stayed behind bars, a cage they call a "wicker." If he saw trouble, he'd pick up an intercom. In short order, a couple dozen goons with bats would show up.

This was a far cry from the kind of accommodations I'd known so far. The Feds put me there because they were trying to RICO me—trying to break me. I had to hand it to them, it was a smart play. If any place could break even the toughest guy, this was it. Dropping me into this dangerous prison was one more way to pressure me to talk. Jon knew that, even if I didn't.

"You have to cooperate," he said. "Otherwise you're gonna get a lot of time and it's gonna be here."

"You gotta get me out of this shithole, man. This is a bad place."

"Are you listening to me, Ted? The Feds are squeezing you to cooperate. If you decide to do it, you have to give them the real deal. You can't lie. If you think you got away with something with the state, that won't happen here. The deal is based on trust, and if they find out you're lying, all bets are off. It would be a disaster. The risk is just too great."

I heard him, but hearing wasn't the same as listening. "You gotta get me out, Jon. Please."

"Until you cooperate I can't do anything. As for the Feds, they're not going to move you to the next bunk, much less another facility."

"Why?"

"Why? They're trying to break you down."

"Fuck them," I said. "This is double jeopardy. They can't come after me twice for the same crime."

"Actually, they can. Double jeopardy means they can't go after you twice in the same jurisdiction. The state got you for it as a state crime. Now the Feds are gonna do you for a federal crime."

"Are you shitting me?"

"You're going to be right here until the end of your state sentence. Then the Feds take over for their case, and they'll move you to a federal penitentiary."

"Fuck that," I said. "I want to go home."

"You don't get to go home, Ted. Not this time." He stood up to leave. "You think about that. You have to talk."

There was no good answer. I could stay here and suffer and maybe get killed, or roll on the people I knew and face another kind of danger.

Those first nights were the roughest. In the bunk below, I heard a guy climb in next to the man already there. I heard fabric across skin, and the flicking sound the waistband of a pair of boxers makes when you pull it over your hips. I heard a grunt and another grunt in response, then the squeak of sorry old springs. Then I heard whispering, then slobbering, then a man trying not to moan. Then I started to cry. It was the first time I could remember doing that since I was a kid.

Two nights later I saw a guy burned alive. Somebody caught him in his bunk, doused him with lighter fluid, and tossed a match. By the time help arrived the guy was done. It looked like what I figured it would. What I hadn't expected was the smell. They say you can't describe the smell of charred flesh but you'll always remember it. This is correct.

Fast-forward a few more days to lunch. Just up the line I saw some guy cut in. A second later, the guy who cut got cut with a shank, a homemade knife. Right in the back. Nearly had the blade pushed through his belly and out his stomach. The guy dropped dead. In no hurry, guards wandered in and hauled him out. The line accommodated the disturbance but never stopped, like ants making room around a rock too big to climb. This kind of thing wasn't rare. A guy getting shanked in the mess room was as remarkable as a guy refilling the saltshakers.

I thought about my choice: stay here and risk being the next guy to get hurt or killed, or get to someplace safer by ratting out the crew. As horrible as it was here, I knew what Ray's guys were capable of. Everybody knew what Ray did to Jimmy Savoy. I decided to stick with the devils I knew. I wouldn't talk. I'd stay here and roll the dice.

Chapter 24

TARGET

Not long after, I connected with someone inside who could help me. Joe Sorrentino was an older guy who also had a connection to Ray. He told me that the business with the stabbing was more important than I realized.

As a martial artist and now a world champ, I figured the intimidation factor would be enough to keep me out of trouble. "Just the opposite," Joe said. "In the schoolyard, the kid who wants attention doesn't beat up the skinny kid. He beats up the toughest kid." I'd learned that firsthand in grade school. Now I'd have to go through the lesson again, and in a dangerous place. The toughest kid was me, and there was a prison yard full of assholes who wanted to find out just how tough. "If anybody does anything against you, even something small, and you don't push back, you're gonna be the one with the problem," he said. "You got two choices, fight or fuck."

I had been setting myself up for a fight and didn't even know it. I did two-mile runs around the huge yard every day, and that was just the warmup. Sometimes I'd be out there with Mercury Morris, the legendary running back from the undefeated Miami Dolphins team of '72, who was doing time for drugs. The other inmates saw all this as showing off, and as a dare to do something about it. It'd been going on for so long that Joe said the gangs would start with the beat-me-to-a-pulp phase and move directly to passing my ass around.

"Pick a fight out of the blue," Joe said. "Otherwise you're gonna get attacked by a gang. They'll do it in the showers. You won't walk away."

"I know how to street-fight," I said.

"Not with a crowd on top of you," he said. "It'll be over before the wicker even sees it. And if they don't kill you, they'll make you their bitch after." He pointed to the yard.

It's hard to imagine, but at some point in the history of prisons, some warden looked out over at a few hundred men who worked out daily for hours on end, men with documented histories of violence who carried irreconcilable, pent-up hostility every minute of the day—the warden who saw all that said, *Let's toss up a boxing ring and let 'em go at each other. What could go wrong?*

"You don't have to wait for 'em to grab you in the shower," Joe said. "You could just go get in the ring." I thought the only way out was blood on concrete. I knew there was legitimate boxing inside but I didn't know anything as civilized as that could settle this.

"Works for me," I said.

"Let's get your ass out there."

You don't pick your prison gang. You go to the one where everybody has your color skin. Here, the Black gang ran the boxing, and the inmate who controlled access to the ring itself was muscled up like crazy and tough as fuck: five-eleven, 220 pounds, sixteen-inch arms. This guy would pick the inmate he wanted to watch fight. Sometimes he'd fight the guy himself. He'd order the guy into the ring or drag him there, then beat the hell out of him. For reasons that were never clear, this imposing African American man went by the name of German.

Joe took me to meet him. "Ted's my boy," Joe said. "I'll put him against you or any one of the motherfuckers in your gang thinks he knows how to box."

I reacted before German could. "Joe, what the hell?"

"I don't care who ya got, German." Now Joe was really selling it. "Big guy, tall guy, my money's on Pryor. You know who Pryor is, don't you?" German looked around at the gang. They knew.

"My money's on my man," Joe said, and he said it with the cocky confidence of someone who wasn't going to have to back up the words himself. Then, just to make it impossible for German to turn us down, he said something else. "My boy will light up any motherfucking one of your niggers."

Now, let's pause for a second. I don't talk like that. Joe was a different story. He was an old Mafia guy. There were a few things that everyone in Belle Glade knew, and one was that Joe Sorrentino was connected so deep that you didn't fuck with him—not for anything he did, not for anything he said, no matter how much he pissed you off. On top of that, he was the go-to man for whatever you wanted on the side. Money, smokes, placing a bet, whatever, Joe could get it. So, Joe could use words like that and get away with it. In his mind, in fact, he was showing you his own kind of respect. If he talked to you like a bad motherfucker, he thought you were a bad motherfucker.

"You want to put up that little white boy? I'll kick his ass myself," said German. Like that, it was on. They put gloves on me but no headgear. This wasn't some curated sparring match. This was full-on street fighting, just in a ring.

Round one was typical. We felt each other out. German was surprised I didn't go down right away. He wasn't used to going against a trained athlete, someone with a strategy beyond swinging like crazy. At the bell—we had a bell—he called over to Joe. "This white boy's pretty good!" he said. The second round, I was getting in my licks and he's getting in his, but now it was clear to me that German was a brawler, not a fighter. If you know the fight game, you know a brawler has a weakness: he's counting on finishing you before he runs out of energy. A brawler can't go the distance, and he lives and dies by the lucky punch that puts you on your back.

And I've never been on my back.

By round three, German was dragging. The best he could hope for was to make it to the bell. I wasn't going to allow that. Joe cared that I would win that way because a knockout would show them all how tough I was. I cared because of that, too, but also because I don't like to lose. I gave German a left hook and a hard right that knocked him senseless. As he folded through the ropes, I finished my combination with a roundhouse kick to the head. He fell five feet to the grass below.

Too late, I found out that winning this one came with its own problems. In an instant, German's gang was in the ring on me. Through the melee, I saw German find his feet again. I covered up under the punches.

"Don't anybody touch that white boy," German shouted. "He's mine." The storm ceased and the seas parted to make way for German. I figured he was going to kill me.

Now Joe jumped in. "German, you son of a bitch, he beat you fair and square. You want a rematch, get your Black ass back in the ring and fight him again," he said. German looked confused.

"Joe, you're crazy. I ain't goin' back up there. That boy is fucking good!" he said. Then he addressed his gang. "Any you niggers touch that white boy, your ass is mine. That boy is golden now, you hear? Touch that boy, you answer to me."

German respected skill, and skill is what I had. I beat him honestly and that was enough. No matter where you go, there's a bit of honor to be found, even in prison. German and I started working out together, usually on the heavy bag. I taught him how to kick, and I introduced him to the martial arts. The fact that we were connected, maybe the two toughest guys in the prison, kept me safe and with dignity. I wasn't his ward and he wasn't my protector. We were on the same side, and no one was going to mess with that.

Chapter 25

EASY RIDER

N ot every prison experience is a terror. Once you settle in, you find rhythms inside that aren't too different from what you know outside, including crossing paths with the rich and famous. It was in prison, after I'd been transferred to the federal prison camp at Eglin Air Force Base, where I met Albert Nipon, sent away for trying to bribe an IRS agent. He started out as an accountant in Philly. In a few years he leveraged the good taste of his wife, Pearl, into a clothing line with famous fans like Rosalynn Carter, Nancy Reagan, and Mary Tyler Moore. Albert served twenty months, sometimes working in the kitchen, sometimes cutting grass like I did.

Then there was Aldo Gucci, sent away at age eighty-one to serve a year and a day for evading $7 million in taxes. He was CEO of the Gucci company and a marketing genius, the man who made his own name into another word for "elegance." When I met him I had no idea who he was, just an old fellow who didn't look like he was going to last long. As the new guy, he had to take the top bunk, but that was going to be hard for him, so I gave him mine on the bottom. Once I understood who he was, I went into bodyguard mode and kept the shakedown types at a distance. It was the right thing to do, and no trouble for me. When we were both out, I took my wife shopping one day at the Palm Beach Gucci store. There was Aldo. He greeted us and waved to one of the clerks. "Take care of my friend," he said. "Don't give him a bill." I'm a little embarrassed to say Tonita walked out of there with shoes and bags worth enough to make a down payment on a small house. She was in heaven, and Aldo was happy to repay the kindness, though I was happy just to have done something in prison for a friend.

Those guys were high profile, and they usually got easy indoor assignments like the laundry or the kitchen. I may have been high profile in the martial arts world, but that didn't mean jack inside. They assigned me to a "cutting crew." I ran a bush hog, which is a mower with blades on hinges that you drag behind a tractor. When you pull it across a stump, the blades yield. That way you can mow any kind of terrain. It takes all your attention to keep it under control. I mowed eight hours a day for twenty-three cents an hour. It wasn't much, but getting paid at all in prison is surprising.

The team I was on worked far enough away from the prison that we could occasionally grab a little freedom. I couldn't spend the day with my wife in my townhouse anymore, but once in a while I could get a half hour of privacy. I'd draw a map for my wife that told her where to meet me, usually out among some trees, and I'd pay off our civilian supervisor, Big Red, to pretend like nothing was happening. Tonita would drive out in a rented station wagon. Why the station wagon? Because you can't stuff a mattress in a sedan. This was my conjugal visit, otherwise unavailable for guys like me. Big Red got $500 for his trouble, and you know what I got.

On top of assigned work, I was running up to ten miles a day and hitting the heavy bag. That meant I was wearing out shoes like crazy, but they wouldn't give me a new pair. So when my brother came to visit every few weeks he'd come in wearing new sneakers. While we talked, we'd kick off our shoes under the table and trade.

Prison was also where I saw one of the funniest things I've seen in my life. This was at the federal prison camp at Eglin Air Force Base, where I'd already crossed paths with Aldo and Albert. My friend Brad Parks worked in the motor pool. What motor pool guys got away with was legendary, and by that I mean I don't know how much of what I heard was true. Start with what was for sure: their job was to take care of cars, which would be the best job you could get in prison. But they also got to work as chauffeurs, including for military officers. On top of that, word was they could get booze whenever they wanted. I can't imagine colonels and majors hopping into a vehicle behind a prisoner, especially one with access to liquor, but that was the story. Whatever the perks were, motor pool guys got off base a lot. They said that, sometimes, if the person you were driving liked you, they would let you catch an hour in a hotel to meet your wife or girlfriend. Better than a rendezvous on a mattress in a station wagon, for sure.

One of the guys who worked with Brad was a funny character we all called Boobus. One day, the assignment was to drive a team of skydivers to a nearby airstrip. Whether Boobus was driving or just riding along is lost to history, but one thing was certain: by the time they got to the airstrip, Boobus was ripped, and ready for an adventure.

Meanwhile, I and the other guys doing landscaping were on our usual thing. We had walkie-talkies so we could keep up with each other and the guards could keep up with us. All of a sudden everybody was on the radio. In the distance, a half dozen sirens started wailing. We didn't know what was going on until somebody looked up.

They were low enough now to be recognized for what they were: five men in gray and black, holding hands to make a ring, falling happily through the sky and seconds away from pulling their rip cords. In the middle of them? Boobus—in a bright orange jumpsuit. The kind prisoners wear, the kind that's not supposed to be on somebody falling from the sky.

The guys had invited Boobus for a little drunk skydiving. He had accepted the challenge despite his status as an involuntary guest of the government, as his uniform displayed. After he touched ground, it took less than a minute for guards to swarm him. They put Boobus in "the hole" overnight, then shipped him away the next day to parts unknown. But for one brief, shining moment, Boobus was a man in the sky, definitely drunk and definitely free.

Chapter 26

DEALER

The Feds had put me here to break me. It hadn't worked.

In the beginning I hadn't known if I could survive in this shithole, but with Joe's advice, German's friendship, and my skills as a fighter, I'd found a way not just to get along but to thrive. All the things they wanted to happen weren't happening. I wasn't walking around scared, wasn't getting beaten by the gangs, wasn't getting fucked in the showers. Just the opposite: I was tight with the toughest guy in the facility, and inside three months I'd become cock of the walk. I'd get up at eight in the morning and spend the day working out, working the bag, and being a rec director with other inmates, even teaching a little martial arts and fighting technique. It's what I would have been doing on the outside. I enjoyed it, I was good at it, and, for me, it was easy.

The Feds' guys on the inside gave them this update, so they turned up the heat. If the federal prosecutors couldn't drive me into a deal by scaring me to death, getting me beaten up, or setting me up to get raped, they'd work me to death. They had me reassigned to the sugar-cane fields.

Now I would be rousted out at 4 AM and shoved on a bus that dumped me and some others at a high-security farm. They shackled us together in teams and gave us each a machete to cut cane, a numbing, physical job that takes your whole body to do. The fields were all muck and stink. Even the dirt seemed "dirtier"—this stuff looked like charcoal and stuck to you all over. Lunch came around nine in the morning, when they'd give us each a bologna sandwich and let us sit for a few minutes in the shade of the bus. Even early, the temperatures got high, fast. Didn't matter. They kept us out there all day, every day.

The heat, the humidity, the physical pain, and the numbing repetition of swinging that blade all day long—I regret to admit that the guys who wanted me to talk had finally found my Achilles' heel. Even with just two weeks left on my sentence, I didn't have anything left. I called Jon. "Just make a deal," I said.

"The only deal they're interested in is one where you talk," he said.

"Fine," I said. "But you gotta get me outta here pretty fucking fast."

"Fast is the hardest part," he said.

"Friday, Jon. I want out by Friday."

"I don't know about Friday," he said.

I explained the shitshow that commenced every day before sunrise. "They're not trying to break me, Jon. They're trying to kill me. If they had somebody shank me, at least it'd be fast."

"They don't want you dead, Ted. They just want you to feel like it."

"Tell 'em it worked," I said.

A week later—past Friday, but not long past—Jon had made the deal, and I accepted. I would plead guilty to one count of conspiracy with a maximum sentence of five years. In exchange, I'd tell them what I knew about the Thompson operation. Like I've said over and over, I didn't know much, but they were certain I did. If this would get me out of here, I'd say anything. I wasn't in much of a position to make demands, but I did hold out for this one: I didn't talk until they got me out of this shithole. They didn't mind. They were in as big a hurry as I was.

They immediately transferred me to federal custody in Miami and began three weeks of daily interviews at the office of the federal prosecutor. I unloaded about everyone they wanted to hear about, or at least everyone I knew: Ray Thompson, Pat Menillo, Bobby Sheer, Mike, some others. I was honest. To the extent I held back anything, it was only to protect myself. I didn't want to alert them to anything they didn't already know about, especially regarding my own operation. Let sleeping dogs lie.

We did the deal just before my state sentence was set to conclude, but the federal government had the right to keep me locked away while they built their case. Fortunately, cooperation bought me a lot of goodwill. The Feds so badly wanted what I had to say that Jon was able to persuade the prosecutors to let me go back on the street while I was cooperating. Until I had to appear in court, in fact, I was released on my own recognizance with no other supervision necessary. I'm told this is a rare arrangement. I don't know if it is or not, but I was grateful. I'd come through. I was back on the street.

The federal case was a mirror of the state case, and I had already been punished. "We have good arguments to persuade the judge not to give you a tough sentence," Jon said. "Judge Nesbitt is tough, but she should show leniency." But even Jon could not anticipate what Judge Nesbitt would end up doing.

Chapter 27

FUCKED ONION

N early a year passed between the day I took my deal and the day for my sentencing. I would stand before Lenore Carrero Nesbitt, United States district judge of the US District Court for the Southern District of Florida. She looked like the model of a professional woman of the time: the stiff hair, the heavy makeup, the big jewelry—these were standard in 1984. She looked serious and not at all casual, like she felt her office deserved someone who looked as imposing as the courthouse itself. Judge Nesbitt was reaching the peak of her career, and handling my part in the Thompson headlines would be valuable to her. I didn't think she liked me but I thought she'd respect the prosecution's deal.

The prosecutor, Brian McCormack, didn't seem to like me, either, but some matters are more important than feelings and he respected fair play. He knew I was being truthful even as he believed I held back on a few things, but he didn't press the issue since he was getting what he wanted. His team of prosecutors originally wanted me to get fifteen years. Thanks to Jon's negotiation, the prosecution agreed to one conspiracy count, which had no mandatory minimum and carried a five-year maximum. With the government praising my cooperation, Jon was hopeful that five years might end up as much less. At sentencing, Brian put in a good word for me, noting my cooperation and that I had built a responsible life on the outside as an athlete. With even the prosecution in my corner, I thought I was in a good position.

With all this support and affirmation in the record, Judge Nesbitt called me to the bench and said something like, "Mr. Pryor, I see all these articles before me, and these claims that you've redeemed yourself, that you're a world champion athlete, that you make appearances on television and in the press, that you have made something out of your life that we should respect, perhaps emulate.

"I don't agree. Mr. Pryor, I think you're a disgrace to children. You are not a mentor. You are a greedy, manipulative person with a lot of connections in the criminal world and a lot of connections in law enforcement. Because of all that, I find that no one has delivered to you the justice that you deserve.

"Mr. Pryor, I'm going to give you something that someone needed to give you a long time ago, a dose of justice. I'm going to impose the full term of your agreement, five years imprisonment. Since you cooperated, I will grant you one year credit.

"Thaddeus Pryor, I sentence you to four years in prison."

This wasn't the plan. Jon immediately jumped in, trying to buy us some breathing room to fix this. "Your honor," Jon said, "I'd like to request a delay. Would you grant my client ninety days to get his affairs in order before he reports to prison?"

Even the prosecutor was surprised. "Your honor, if Mr. Pryor needs ninety days, we don't mind," said Brian.

"I mind," said Judge Nesbitt. "Mr. Pryor, you go to jail today." And I did. They cuffed me and led me out of the courtroom. Years later, I'd hear a courthouse story that explained it. The word was that when she first took the federal bench after her time serving the state, she said to the other judges, "I'm gonna teach you boys how to sentence."

Less than an hour after she'd personally demonstrated her philosophy to me, I was, for the third time in my life, in prison-intake processing. From there, they'd send me to Federal Prison Camp at Eglin Air Force Base in Pensacola.

Chapter 28
LAST MAN STANDING

That should have been the end of the story. My part in the investigation was done, and we'd somehow kept our operation off the front pages. In less than ten years I had put away money—call it a rainy-day fund. Four years from that time, sooner with parole, I'd walk out of prison and collect. All I had to do was wait. Then, a month before I was set for work release, it all went sideways one last time.

In 1983, my partner Scott Errico had flown to England with a suitcase full of drug money and the name of one man, Patrick Diamond, who would meet him at the airport and carry in the cash under his diplomatic passport. He had schooled Scott in laundering large amounts of cash, and that education consisted of learning one name, Shaun Murphy. Shaun was an accountant working low-regulation, high-dollar banking in the British Virgin Islands and the Isle of Man. He laundered money not just for Ray but for anybody in the smuggling game who could find him. Shaun was the linchpin, the last step. He took the money to banks in the region who would accept massive cash deposits in exchange for a processing fee, no questions asked. Dirty money comes in and clean money comes out at the price of a few percentage points. Scott, IndyCar driver Randy Lanier, Dennis McGuire, Patrick Bilton, myself, and other smugglers outside of Ray's business moved their money through there.

The problem was that Scotland Yard had been watching the whole thing. They arrested Diamond, then picked up Scott. A little push was all it took to get Scott to call attorney Michael Levine, Patrick Bilton's point man on laundering cash. Agents listened in. Things went downhill fast. Scotland Yard raided Murphy's offices and took his files, which were a Rosetta Stone for US drug-money laundering. PBS's *Frontline*, which investigated all this, said that Murphy and Diamond had accounting records for all occasions: one set to show to their clients, one for the auditors, and one with the real numbers.

There's nothing illegal about keeping accounts in the British Virgin Islands and the Isle of Man, but few people would keep money there if they intended to pay taxes on it. This is what brought investigators back to me, but there was more. They knew where the money had come from, meaning our years of smuggling would be exposed. This thing would put me away for the rest of my life, but that's where the twist comes in. They would be willing to forget it all if I'd tell them what they wanted to know.

They had decided the triggerman on Jimmy Savoy's murder was Scott. The word had long been that he was one of Ray's enforcers. I'd known him forever and worked with him up close. I'd also been in the room when Ray sent his goons out to bring back Jimmy Savoy, the room where I said I'd have nothing to do with killing, the room where

Ray cursed me until I walked away forever. I'd spent plenty of hours in the company of men who weren't afraid of getting physical, but Scott I knew well. I had always doubted the enforcer talk and had never been able to imagine him as a murderer. We hadn't had contact in years. Didn't matter. They wanted me to help find him, an anonymous fugitive last seen in the south of France, and they wanted me to name him as the killer. One more time, they were asking me for something I didn't know.

One day a couple guards pulled me out of general population and dropped me in solitary. I didn't know what the fuck was going on and nobody would say. After thirty days they let me out and Jon Sale showed up. Whatever they were softening me up for, the Feds had made him the messenger. "Tell me about this money in the Isle of Man," he said. If Jon was asking, that meant the Feds had found my money and were taking it all. Years of risk, years of work, and time in prison, all for nothing.

My fortune was erased.

"Money in the Isle of Man, Ted?" he asked again.

"Mystery to me, Jon. I got nothing for you."

"Don't lie to me," he said. "You're safe telling me anything—and you need to. It's confidential. I'm here to keep you out of trouble. If you sit there like you don't know anything, they're going to wrap you up in a RICO prosecution, tie you to organized crime, tie you to everything Ray's outfit ever ran. Doesn't matter what you didn't do. If they did it, it's like you did it, too."

"Yeah."

"You remember how you felt after six weeks of cutting sugarcane? Try twenty-five to life, Ted. Try maximum security. They pulled you out of solitary and that was only thirty days."

"I don't have money in the Isle of Man."

Jon had once been frightened for me. This went beyond that. "Ted, I'm not telling you this as your lawyer. I'm telling you as a friend," he said. "This is the end. They're giving you one opportunity. Last time you didn't cooperate, they put you in prison. This time, they're gonna throw away the key. If you have money in the Isle of Man, they already know it."

I had gone from waiting for my fortune to losing it all, and now I was negotiating to avoid prison for the rest of my life. All they wanted in exchange was information I didn't have.

"What do you want me to do?"

"Full cooperation. You trade that for no jail time. I can get that." And just when I thought we'd hit bottom, he played one last card. "They want you, Ted. But they're about one more ask away from giving the deal to Mike instead."

Mike was Michael Levine. If I didn't make a deal before Levine cracked, they'd have no reason not to bury me. Hell, they'd enjoy it, finally nailing me after only getting close before. "You know Mike," said Jon. "He'll crack before they ask him his name." I laughed because it was true.

"Yeah, that's funny," said Jon. "Then he's out walking around and you're the one in prison forever. You let it come to that, these prosecutors are gonna do you for the hell of it."

"Yeah," I said.

"Then again, Patrick might beat you and Mike both to it. And he's gonna roll on you. Patrick nearly got you killed in Jamaica. You're gonna let him take your deal? They want him more than they want you so they can nail down the Brinks thing." Patrick had been one of the guys who laundered the money from the famous 1983 Brinks robbery at Heathrow Airport. The Feds couldn't prove it, but if they could nail him on my case, they could use it as leverage on that case.

Jon paused to let it all sink in. "I'm going to ask you one more time, Ted. How much did you have in the Isle of Man?"

There was no longer any reason to pretend. I told him. "Twenty-five million."

"That's gone," Jon said, as if I hadn't figured it out. "It's every man for himself now, Ted, and the Feds are making deals."

"Whoever jumps on the bus first . . ." I said.

"That's the one who gets to ride," he said. "The only one."

"Gimme a week," I said.

"You don't have a week. Either one of those guys could've rolled while we're sitting here talking."

"One week," I said. Jon didn't argue any more. I'm pretty sure he knew what I was thinking. If I did a deal but came out of prison with everything gone, I might as well stay in prison forever. I needed a soft landing.

I connected with friends on the outside to hide as much in cash and assets as I could. Even getting to use the phone was a task, mostly bribing guys who could get to one. A few things were still playing out, but I quickly saw that I wouldn't get paid. The biggest: Mike had ten thousand pounds of my marijuana to sell, product he owed me $5 million for. I never saw the money, though he saw the inside of a jail cell for a decade.

The outlook was so grim that at one point I decided I'd disappear. We were experts at smuggling marijuana. It wasn't a big stretch that we could smuggle a person. I would spend the rest of my life a fugitive. The heat would die down in a few years, but I could never return to the United States. I'd have to keep one eye over my shoulder, always. I almost did it, almost, but I couldn't bail on my family. My brother had always been my hero. He didn't deserve for me to disappear. Neither did my father. I couldn't make him spend the rest of his life with a son on the run.

Then time ran out. Word came that Patrick was making a deal and his confession included me. I couldn't tell the Feds the thing they wanted to hear me say, but if they wanted me so bad, maybe cooperating would be enough. I told Jon to tell them I was all in.

Over the next two months, they pulled me out of my cell every few days for a ten-hour bus ride to Miami and secret go-rounds with the FBI, the Secret Service, the DEA, and any other agency that wanted a piece of me. They quickly decided I was telling the truth when I said I knew nothing about Scott and the murder, or maybe they were getting information from elsewhere that made my part less important. Whatever it was, they took full advantage to ask me about other things. I answered every question they asked and told them everything I could remember. I gave up the details of our smuggling operation and how I got my take even while I was in prison. It was as close to a full confession as I ever provided.

They also wanted me to tell them if their years of hunches had been right. Some were, some weren't. For instance, they couldn't figure how I'd beaten the rap the first time with Judge Kaplan, so they had decided that someone may have bribed him on my behalf. They were wrong. Judge Kaplan was an honest man who got overturned not because he took a bribe to decide in my favor but because a judge above him had priorities besides the law.

No one inside man ever laid out the whole Ray Thompson operation. I'm not sure any one guy could have. Nearly everybody in the organization rolled on somebody, and nearly everybody was made to pay. A few guys got to walk away clean, including my brother. Since he could verify that everything I said was true, that made him valuable and allowed me to keep him from an indictment. Otherwise, sentences ran from ten to twenty years all the way to life. What you ended up with depended on when you finally hopped on that bus to start talking. I got on early, while I still had information they could use. Others waited too long, their stories already put on the record by somebody else.

But me? I talked. And I walked.

Chapter 29

UNDERDOG

With no more charges coming out of this final round, I figured I was finally in the home stretch. I should have known better. They weren't finished with me at all. The biggest risks still lay ahead. To put it in boxing terms, I had two fights left, and I'd have to win them both. Call it the championship doubleheader for the title belt.

When you get caught doing anything illegal, one thing prosecutors want to do is separate you from the profits. They'd already separated me from the money I'd stashed in the Caribbean. (The federal government, which absorbed these funds, spends about $200,000 a second. They spent what I'd saved faster than it takes to have a sneezing fit.) Now they had found a little more and they wanted that, too.

Which brings me to Fight #1, the undercard.

For years I had kept Tonita out of all this. I didn't want her to have to deal with our business, didn't want her to have to make difficult choices, and I didn't want her to worry about me. Most of all I didn't want her to have to lie. Sometimes I made things more difficult for myself than they had to be just to keep her clean. Now that I was approaching the end of this, I'd find out if I'd protected her enough.

Patrick and I had separately made deals, known as proffers, with the prosecutors, exchanging information for a better shot at getting out of trouble. Individually we shared what we'd done and what we thought other people had done. Our stories matched up because we were telling the truth. The problem came when they asked us about assets. They'd already bled me dry over the Isle of Man, and those assets were now out in the open. But I also had a small amount of cash that nobody knew about except for Patrick and me. I left it out of my proffer, but Patrick mentioned it in his.

I set that cash aside for a simple reason: I wanted a nest egg for when I was released from prison. To keep Tonita out of trouble, I told her nothing about it. Instead, I'd had my share of profits delivered to her mother. Unless the investigators had been staking out Tonita's mom, that would be where the story ended. If Tonita was asked about money, she could truthfully say she knew nothing.

That set up the showdown. I said there was no money, Patrick said there was money, and it would be my word against his. The only person who could settle it would be someone prosecutors didn't know to call, Tonita's mother. If they figured out her presence in any of this and asked her about the money, my proffer would be torn up—they're no good if there's a lie in there—and I could have gone to prison for ten to life. But they didn't know to ask Tonita's mother. The only one they knew to ask was Tonita.

I didn't want her to have to testify at all. When I say she'd already endured what she didn't deserve, I mean that down to the letter. The authorities had confiscated everything we had. They had taken our house and thrown her out of it. Our bank accounts? Gone. Our property, even things like furniture and cars? So long to that, too. If we owned it before, we didn't own it anymore. She had put up with all of that and stood by me. And now she was going to be subpoenaed to go in front of a grand jury.

"She's suffered enough, Jon. You gotta keep her out of it," I said.

"No way to keep her out of it," Jon said. "They're gonna force her to testify."

"Can you at least represent her?"

"I can't do that, either. I'm already representing you. It's a conflict." He told me to get her Vinnie Flynn, a powerhouse criminal lawyer we both knew, Jon from the courthouse and me from the fight scene. He wasn't just a pro. He was a friend we could count on. But we had no guarantees that her questioning wouldn't yield some awful surprise. I never told Jon Sale or Vinnie Flynn that Tonita's mother was hiding my cash. I did not tell them because they would not suborn perjury, and anyway, I would not have asked them to do so. Tonita had immunity but the deal didn't cover perjury. My staying out of prison now depended on how well I'd kept her in the dark. Now I'd find out if I really had closed all the exits.

They grilled Tonita for hours. If courtroom questioning can feel unfair, at least both sides will eventually be heard. Not so with a grand jury. The prosecutor can present the harshest case possible because he has no enforceable obligation to present both sides or even to be fair.

No defense attorney is present. Ever heard the old saying that a prosecutor can get a grand jury to indict a ham sandwich? It's true, and that's why.

Tonita testified truthfully: she had no knowledge of the money. That meant this came down to Patrick's word against hers. That was the best possible outcome because in that competition, Tonita had the upper hand. No fancy footwork from the prosecutor could change the fact that Patrick was a felon, while Tonita had no record at all. On top of that, Patrick had already offered up stories before that didn't pan out, like the business with the Marine Patrol and the three keys of coke on the boat we had run up on the sandbar.

The grand jury declined to indict. My wife walked away clean. That meant I walked away clean, too.

I had dodged not just a bullet but a missile, that ten-to-life sentence. I owe my freedom to her. Which brings me to Fight #2, the main event.

They also wanted my house in Vail, Colorado. I had told them about it, but I'd said I hadn't bought it with money from smuggling. That made it something I could keep. Once again, Patrick said otherwise, so they decided to challenge me on that, too. Having failed to get me on the cash with Tonita, they intended to renege on their proffer and take one last shot at me.

Prosecutor Brian McCormack had been reasonable in the past. He had even put in a good word for me when Judge Nesbitt put me on full blast. Now he was mad. I think he was frustrated that I had never been sentenced to any big run of hard time. Like a lot of prosecutors, he knew a lot of things that couldn't be mentioned in court, so it must have been especially frustrating to see me walk on previous cases. I believe he saw my freedom as the outcome of manipulating the system, pure and simple. Of course, nearly nothing had really gone my way. At best, I'd been able to shave off the roughest edges of a bad situation. And I still carried that grudge against Nancy Reagan's "Just Say No" campaign, which had fed the public obsession with all this by making no distinction between weed and hard drugs.

Unless I could prove I was telling the truth, it would be more than just losing the house. The end of the proffer would be the end of my freedom, probably for the rest of my life.

"I can do this," I said.

"Are you fucking crazy?" said Jon. "You're gonna risk everything for a lousy house that's not even worth much? You're gonna perjure yourself?"

I told Jon not to worry, that I wasn't going to perjure myself.

"It's a polygraph test. If you lie, they indict you all over again. You want to risk reopening everything that we've already made go away?" He insisted I not go along. "They can't force you to take it," said Jon.

"It's this or nothing," I said.

"Or you could just let go of the house. If this goes south . . ." He let that hang in the air, then squared off with me, sort of like you would do if you were about to start a fight. "Ted, how many times have you been at this point? You know, where if you lose they'll put you under the jail? How many?"

I let him have his say. Once again, as with my Isle of Man money, Jon was talking not only as my lawyer but also as my friend, desperate to keep me from risking a mistake I couldn't come back from.

"You did get the money from smuggling, right?"

"Jon, I did not get the money from smuggling." To tell the truth, to this day, I'm not sure. I had smuggling money but I also had legitimate income.

"You sure about that? You can't beat a polygraph," he said. But I was determined to try. I had one weapon left in the arsenal, one I hadn't had reason to use much in all this, but now it was the only thing that could save my house, my future, my freedom, everything.

When you are a serious practitioner of the martial arts, you also become a serious practitioner of meditation. I have meditated for thousands of hours. I meditated in prison. I meditate every day, to this day. During meditation, you enter a state of heightened concentration. Do this daily for years and it is eventually accompanied by a level of control over the body that is impossible to achieve any other way.

At that point in my meditation practice, I had long possessed profound control over my body. If I felt an itch on my leg, I could make it go away just by going into that trancelike state. (It would be easier just to reach down and scratch it, but you get the point.) More importantly, I could raise or lower my blood pressure, body temperature, and more.

A lie detector tests four things: how rapidly you breathe, your blood pressure, your heart rate, and how much you sweat. A polygraph examiner is looking for one or more of those values to go up when you give an answer. This makes immediate sense: when you lie, you get tense, and when you get tense, all of these things tick upward. If you want to beat a polygraph, you have to be able to control those things. If you're a serious practitioner of meditation, you can.

On the day of the test, they sat me in a wooden chair and the operator connected a half dozen sensors to my fingers, chest, and a few other places. Last, he put a blood pressure cuff around my arm, turned on the machine, and went into an adjoining room. The examiner wasn't the only one in there, either. Jon was there, still wishing I'd turned this down, and the prosecutor was there, too, maybe to try to make me even more nervous. I was alone, just me and the machine. And the test began.

The examiner started with simple questions to establish baseline readings: my name, the date, if I knew who the president was, that sort of thing. But he quickly moved on to the questions that mattered.

EXAMINER: Do you own a house in Vail, Colorado?
ME: Yes.
EXAMINER: Is this property in your name?
ME: Yes.
EXAMINER: Did you take out a loan to purchase this house?
ME: No.
EXAMINER: Have you engaged in the smuggling of marijuana?
ME: Yes.
EXAMINER: Have you made money from smuggling?
ME: Yes.
EXAMINER: Did you purchase the house in Vail with proceeds from smuggling?
ME: No.
EXAMINER: Are you also a professional kickboxer?
ME: Yes.
EXAMINER: Have you made money from kickboxing?
ME: Yes.
EXAMINER: Did you purchase the house in Vail with proceeds entirely from kickboxing or other legal activities?
ME: Yes.

That was the big question, the reason we were there. My answer was false because of one word, "entirely." The house was purchased with money partly from legal activities and probably partly from smuggling. To this day, I'm not sure how much came from each.

With the big hurdle crossed, now he asked the same questions in a different order, phrased them a little differently, sometimes with a different tone of voice or at a different speed. Then it was over. The door opened. The examiner walked into the exam room followed by the two attorneys. It was clear they didn't know the outcome any more than I did. The examiner disconnected me from the machine. Now the three of us stood close to him, ready for the news.

"He passed," said the examiner.

"He passed?" said the prosecutor.

"He passed."

"I passed," I said.

"What do you mean, he passed?" said the prosecutor.

"He passed," said Jon.

"How in the world did he do that?"

"Sir, I have two jobs, to administer the test and to interpret it," said the examiner. "This one isn't even a close call. You wanna look at the paper yourself?"

I didn't rub it in but I wanted to.

"I don't know what the fuck he was doing," said the examiner. "Rolled his eyes into the back of his head. Completely white. Freakiest thing I ever saw. But he passed."

The words hadn't left the man's mouth before the prosecutor was in my face. "Is this some kind of kung fu trick, Pryor?"

"Sir," I said, "all I did was answer the truth."

"The hell you did," said the prosecutor.

"This was your idea, not mine," I said—again, calmly, and I could easily be calm because I knew I had won. "You said I could keep my house, you wrote it in the proffer, then you went back on your word. You could have believed me instead of Patrick, but you decided to come down on me. I didn't like that, but I went along. Then you said if I passed the polygraph, I could keep my house. I didn't like that, but I went along again. Now I passed the test and you want to change the rules one more time? With all due respect, sir, you're more interested in getting the outcome you want than in playing by the rules—or keeping your own word."

The prosecutor was not happy. The prosecution team was not happy. I was very happy. I had won both fights. No apologies, no regrets. Winner and still champion.

Chapter 30

FREE MAN

In the spring of 1985 I walked out of prison a free man. I'd never go
there again, and I'd never go back to the smuggling business, either.
As for the rest of the guys from the business in Miami and beyond,
the way it came out wasn't a matter of justice, because justice is in the
eye of the beholder. I think it was a matter of being fortunate or not,
smart or not, and clever or blessed or both.

A few made a fortune and never got discovered. Good for them.
I've kept them out of this tale so far and I won't out them now. Some
got caught and trimmed their time or avoided prison completely by
telling what they knew or repeating what they were told to say. Others
did the time without mercy. Then they got out and put it all in the
rearview. If you met them today you wouldn't know they were a part of
this wild story unless you knew exactly what to look for in some dusty
newspaper archive. They've earned their anonymity, so I'll leave them

be, too. Two felt the full force of the law, though. Ray was one of them. He deserved it. But the other, I think he did not.

In 1990 the State of Florida tried Scott Errico for a role in the double murder Ray had ordered ten years prior. I didn't think Scott did it, didn't think he was capable of it. The original plan was for me to testify against him, but that fell through because I had nothing to say. Instead, when the trial finally came around and my legal troubles were settled, I testified on Scott's behalf. The judge was Stan Kaplan, the man who'd presided over my own case. As I took the stand, the judge and I engaged in a little conversation, a cordial, familiar back-and-forth. It had been a while since we'd seen each other, but he'd kept up with me. He complimented me on my early success in businesses and on my five-year run as world champion. Not a word about my time in front of him as a defendant. This went on in front of the jury, who saw that the man about to testify to Scott's upstanding character had earned the admiration of a judge.

"I don't know anything about the shooting," I said, and it was the truth. "I wasn't around." I told the jury only what I knew for sure, that I'd seen Scott at his best and worst. "He's a good man. If anybody deserves the benefit of a doubt, it'd be him. I can't tell you about a murder. I can't even tell you if he was really on the boat where it happened. All I know for sure is that a lot of people have said a lot of things about all this, and for a lot of reasons that don't have anything to do with justice."

The jury came back with eleven votes to acquit and one holdout for conviction. It took a second trial to put him in prison. He turned down a plea deal and ended up with two consecutive life sentences. He'll be eligible for parole when he's eighty-two if he makes it that long.

We still talk. He's made an exemplary life behind bars, studying to become a minister and then serving as one to the people inside who need some hope. He is now a truly selfless man. I don't think Scott did what he was accused of, and I don't think justice is served by keeping him behind bars, especially at this late date.

Ray Thompson pleaded guilty to ordering those two murders, but the seventeen-year sentence he received would be the least of his problems. When Ray skipped on Miami in 1982, he moved home to Illinois, where he had put some of the operation's drug money into a family restaurant called the Farm Inn. Ray made it the new boathouse. The newspapers said it was the only family restaurant with a four-hundred-pound bodyguard out front wearing gold chains and a sidearm. On January 4, 1985, a scrum of law enforcement agents descended on the Farm Inn and placed Ray under arrest.

The federal government auctioned the marina he'd originally purchased for a million dollars, now worth $5.5 million. They sold off his home south of Fort Lauderdale, too, plus a yacht and condos. It's easy to imagine that without Ray around, more than a little of his stuff never made it to the auction, with beneficiaries on both sides of the law. After all, it was still Miami.

The next year, a jury convicted Ray of conspiracy to import and distribute marijuana, and he pleaded guilty to filing a false tax return to hide $90,000 in drug income. It was chicken feed to Ray, what you could find in his couch cushions, but that's all it took. And the hits kept coming: he received a life sentence under the federal "drug kingpin" law, and, in a separate trial, he was sentenced to the electric chair for the Savoy murder by none other than Judge Stan Kaplan himself.

The jury had come back with a recommendation of life in prison. Judge Kaplan found that to be "unreasonable"—that's the word he used—and upped it to the death penalty. This time the appeals court saw the wisdom in the judge's decision and denied the appeal. Two decades later Ray died in prison, his mind gone.

Chapter 31

THE GUY WHO STARTED OVER

As for me, I started my life again, this time on the straight and narrow. But I was facing one big problem: How in the hell was I going to make a living? If it was going to take a college degree, I'd be shit out of luck. I'd barely made it out of high school. Plus I had a criminal record. But I quickly realized something important. The years of kickboxing and smuggling and navigating in and around the law weren't just a write-off on my way to the straight life. These experiences would give me the skills I'd need to create a legitimate career later, assuming I survived the trip.

All this time, I had been learning how to persuade people. I had spent thousands of hours in front of boxing crowds, cameras, and shady characters. That gave me an instinct for getting them to say yes (or getting them to put down the .45 auto or the Bren Ten or the SIG Sauer P220). I had also been learning how to do business. There's a reason some criminals are wealthy. It's not just because they're breaking the rules. The guys who succeed in crime spend less time on the run-and-gun than they do dealing with the people who work for them and poring over this week's numbers. (Don't believe me? Spend a little time watching *The Sopranos* or *Breaking Bad*. The heavies spend hours with lawyers and accountants.)

The biggest difference between a legitimate and an illegitimate operation is literally that. In terms of the day-to-day stuff they're pretty much the same. You have to know how to structure deals, work with partners, set prices, borrow, invest, keep track of inventory, hire wisely, make good use of your resources, solve problems, and find inefficiencies so you can stop your money from leaking out.

An entrepreneur is an entrepreneur no matter what he's doing. That was me. I had the ability but no credential. It didn't take more than a few rejected applications for me to see that no one was going to hire me. I wasn't used to hearing "no," so I stopped asking. I decided to build a business for myself, only this time I'd do it all aboveboard. I didn't know what kind of business I was going to get into, but as usual, I was confident beyond what most people thought was realistic. I intended to be bigger than I'd ever been. I planned to make more money than I'd ever made and be respected inside and outside of my industry, whatever industry that turned out to be.

I wasn't doing it to prove myself to anybody. Who did I care to impress? Picking fights with long odds is what makes me feel alive. It's what I do. This would be entirely for me.

I talked to a friend in real estate. He showed me the step-by-step on setting up a business with all the licenses and legitimacy it takes. I hired an accountant and made sure he'd keep me legal. Over the course of a couple weeks, my friend gave me a complete graduate-school course in business. I quickly realized that I already had most of that education from running a multimillion-dollar smuggling operation. I was good to go. All I needed was an opening.

With perfect timing, my brother-in-law told me he'd come across an opportunity in the car wash business. It was as good a place as any to begin, it was open to a guy like me, and he was family. I decided to give it a go.

There was only one problem: I didn't have anywhere near enough cash to buy a car wash, let alone build one. I had no assets to borrow against. I was going to have to use those street smarts. I'd have to talk my way in, talk my way through the plan, and talk a developer to the bottom line. All I needed was one adventurous entrepreneur to listen. He'd have to have deep pockets, and he'd have to be more of a speculator than a straight-up investor. That ruled out most of the pack right away. More than anything, I needed someone whose record of investments suggested they were willing to take a chance on someone like me. Eventually, I set my sights on a guy named Morgan Russell.

My initial campaign consisted of calling him every day, sometimes as often as ten times a day. Weeks went by with no answer until one day his secretary put me through. "I'm talking to you to tell you I don't want you to keep calling me anymore. Stop this," he said.

"First of all, thanks for taking my call. And I understand. But do me a favor," I said.

"No, whoever you are. I've taken your call, so stop calling."

"Then don't do me a favor. Do us both a favor. Let me come in and have a meeting with you and show you the idea I have—the reason I've been calling," I said.

"I don't want a meeting with you. I want you to stop calling."

"I get that. Thank you for being direct. But here's the thing: if you don't take the meeting, I'm going to keep calling you until you do."

"Damn," he said, and then a few other things, mostly amazed that some stranger had the stones to push back like that. Anybody else in my position would have sounded like an asshole, but, like I said, I had picked up some skills. I had spent years holding my own against gangsters, working with them side by side, even flat-out making them my friends. I knew I could get Morgan where I needed him to be, and I knew someday he'd thank me for it.

He was older, accomplished, and a tough nut to crack—but the next time he opened his mouth, it was to put me on his calendar.

When I got in front of him, I explained what I had in mind, starting with how it fit in with what he was already doing. Morgan had multiple business projects built around car services. I proposed that he add a car wash to one of them, then rent the place back to me on a long-term lease. I'd guarantee him the same rate of return he'd get if he put his money in a bank. If you think about that for a minute, you realize I wasn't offering much of a deal, since a real bank could guarantee what I was only promising. Morgan would have no incentive to take my offer except for one thing: I'd add an extra 10 percent—the vig, the *vigorish*, the term gamblers use for the little guarantee the house takes against loss. An edge.

In business, that's as good a return as you're gonna find, but it all comes down to how much risk you can take on and not drive yourself crazy worrying about it. The answer depends on this: Do you trust the guy sitting across from you? One more time in my life, it was a matter of whether somebody believed in Ted.

"This has to be the worst financial thing I've done in my career," he said to me. "You have no assets. You have no significant cash. You have a house, but I don't want to have to take your house. You're not bankable, Ted. You're just not bankable. But . . ."

"But," I said, "there's that ten percent."

"Yeah, but I'm not gonna let that cloud my judgment." Then he said, "You're a lot like me, kid. I look at the numbers first, but then I listen to my gut. I like you." He paused, then offered me a handshake. "Let's do it."

And we did. I was no more than a couple years out of prison and I was in business. Over the next seven years, I would open twenty more locations.

Chapter 32

CHAMP

The straight life was beautiful. I had money, respect, and prestige. Of course, I'd had all those things before, but this was better. Now I didn't have to look over my shoulder for somebody coming to take it away. But here's the thing: when you've lived the kind of life I've lived, you're gonna stay hungry. It's like my great friend, the advertising giant Jordan Zimmerman, says, "Never rest in the glory." I never do. In fact, I don't have a choice. I'm driven to do the next thing. So I wasn't looking over my shoulder. I was looking beyond the horizon.

By 1986, I had been out of prison more than a year. I was climbing the ladder again but not without bruises. Tonita had stood by me while I was away. She came to visit me inside and she kept me from being alone. I was committed to doing right by my wife even from behind bars. I loved her, and not only was she standing by me, she'd saved my ass. I made sure the money I'd set aside got doled out to her every month. She got a job to supplement that money, and those two incomes kept her afloat.

Still, it had been a hard comedown for her. The houses, the cars, the cash—the lifestyle she'd had was gone, same as mine. Now she was working a thousand times harder for a thousand times less. When I came out of prison, she asked me for a divorce. I can't say I was surprised. I wanted her to stay and start over with me, but she'd been through a lot and deserved to have what she wanted. It hurt bad to lose her, but to this day she's my hero and remains one of my best friends.

Once I was back on the outside, I didn't waste a day. Every bit of energy I'd put into smuggling and kickboxing, I was now directing toward my new business. I was ferocious at it, I was good at the planning and the execution, and I was loving every minute of it. For my first couple years outside, my attention was 100 percent on business, little else.

Funny thing about life, though: it happens while you're making other plans. One afternoon I was checking out office space for rent in Fort Lauderdale, when I got in the elevator with a beautiful young woman, Lisa Weissman. She was charming—wonderful. We started chatting and from that out-of-the-blue moment in an office building, we went to dinner, and ended up dating for quite some time. Lisa also made a connection for me that would change my life. As we were getting to know each other, I mentioned my car wash business, and she said I should talk to her father, Michael Weissman, who was a very successful entrepreneur. I did, and the rest is history.

Michael would become a mentor to me. He had created a business called Tutor Time, a chain of childhood education centers ranging from infancy through kindergarten. He had built it on franchising and it was huge—more than two hundred locations in twenty-five states and four countries. I didn't know the franchising game, but Michael had my attention. It was also an interesting reverse version of what I'd been doing. I had gotten investors to believe in me. Michael and his son Richard got investors to believe in themselves.

Turns out there are lots of would-be entrepreneurs who don't have the money to buy into something like a McDonald's or a UPS Store, but they absolutely could swing the smaller loan or self-investment to buy into Tutor Time. That's how Michael kicked down the door for them. They could buy a franchise in his childhood education business because, ultimately, it was a price they could afford. It was genius because it was so simple. Before, they couldn't afford to get in, but now they could. Everybody wins. I admired the hell out of it, and I admired the hell out of Michael and Richard. Richard and I got to know each other even better when we went in together on another project, my second car-wash company, American Turbo Wash. He brought the franchise know-how; I brought the experience from my car wash business.

The 1990s were great. Michael became like a second father to me. His wonderful wife, Linda, became like a second mother. And his son, Richard, was like another brother, and has been very successful in business. Michael knew I had chosen to change my life, and he'd watched me do it successfully. He understood the challenge better than a lot of people because before he became an entrepreneur, he'd been in the securities business, where friends can be fickle and any misstep can follow you for the rest of forever. He knew what it felt like to need someone to have a little faith in you. He appreciated my honesty and my achievement. In exchange, he gave me his friendship and a shot at something big. He also gave me a major education in yet more aspects of business, plus a role in the operation where I could put it to use.

He invited me to buy into Tutor Time and I did, taking the role of executive vice president and negotiating deals that helped expand the business.

That's about the time things unraveled again—but it also set me up for the win that would cap all three of my careers and set me up for the rest of my life.

It's easy to believe that all you do is build a big business, then sit back and watch it run itself. That's not how it goes. A big business is like a shark: if it's not moving forward, it's gonna die. You're either rising or falling, and my job was to keep us on the rise—more investment, more resources, more outlets, more everything. It was going so well that we were on our way to the usual destination for a successful business, an IPO—an initial public offering, or "going public."

An IPO is one of the most complex and protracted transactions in business, but it's pretty simple to explain. You divide the ownership of the company into shares, then you sell those shares to investors on everyone's confidence that the company will continue to grow. In time, that can translate into dividends—basically interest paid on your investment—and an increase in the value of your shares. Simple to describe, sure, but doing it involves going through a maze that can take years to navigate.

Most of the things I've done in life I've done on my own, but this is one thing you can't. It takes all kinds of experts, some on your side and a whole lot more on the side of the Securities and Exchange Commission. To get to an IPO, their accountants and lawyers give your company a proctology exam. To navigate all that, you have to work hand in glove with major banks and some of the largest accounting firms in the world. Their job, so it says in the law, is to be sure that investors can trust you.

Trust. There was that word again. I'd built my business career entirely on trust. People who trusted me—with their money and with their confidence—were rewarded with profit. Now I was going to have to win the trust of major banks and accounting firms. That's a different game.

The players in high finance are gatekeepers to a very inside club, and they don't open their doors easily. You could present them with spotless books like we had and the lowest-risk opportunity in the history of the world and it might not be enough. That's because, for them, it's not only about the money, or the profit, or the payoff. It's also about prestige. There are just some kinds of people they don't do business with. People like me.

It's not that these boys have a problem doing business with criminals. Hell, they do that all the time. It's that they like their criminals to already be on the inside of high finance. I wasn't even a criminal anymore, but I was definitely on the outside.

When we were ready to do an IPO, we approached the major accounting firms to guide us through. We got back nothing but *no. No* from the banks. *No* from the accountants. *No* from everybody in the money business. They wanted everybody and everything squeaky clean. They didn't like that Michael had been involved in the rough-and-tumble world of securities in the 1970s, and they sure as hell didn't like me, a convicted felon, in the C-suite. Our success didn't matter. We were the wrong kind of people.

There's a line in the movie *The Godfather* where Michael Corleone, son of the Godfather himself, says *It's not personal. It's strictly business.*

But if you read the book that the movie was based on, you'll find the original line, and it tells a different story, the reality of the situation known to anybody in business: *Don't let anybody kid you. It's all personal, every bit of business. They call it business, but it's personal as hell.*

To clear the playing field for the business to expand, I left Tutor Time. So did Michael. I took two years of salary and a handful of childcare centers, Michael took his part, and we went our separate ways, building the same kinds of businesses under new leadership and new names. He started his own company and I started Children of America.

One more time I get to say it: it was the best damn thing that could have happened. In the years since, I've led my company to becoming the seventh largest childcare provider in the country, with 2,500 employees and 65 locations in 25 states. Those Wall Streeters can keep their IPO. As I sit in my home in Hawaii, things look okay to me.

In 2020, my big brother Tony passed away. We'd started working—really working—together when we were teenagers, kids even, and we kept at it the rest of our lives. He was there when we were dodging trouble from the law and the guns, he was there when we got away with it, he was there when I got sent away, and he was there when I traded the boats and the cash-counting machines for the boardroom. In the end we were together at Children of America. He was running the facilities, hands on.

There's trust, then there's love, then there's blood. Tony, my hero—we had all that, with never a doubt between us. He was there for every story I've told here, and every story that'll stay between just us forever. He was there for me, always. I think he still is.

People change. I smuggled pot and went to prison for it. That was forty years ago, and the Small Business Administration still won't let me in the door. Meanwhile, I went on to build a chain of the most successful childhood education centers in America. Parents trust me with the most precious people in their lives, their children. I achieved that not in spite of what I went through but because of it. I got to keep the best parts of who I am.

I wish the story of building my business came with as many crazy tales as kickboxing and smuggling did, but it doesn't. Nobody in my world these days knows what it's like to end up bound in zip ties next to a table full of cocaine in a Jamaican hideout. These days the closest calls I have are with green-eyeshade types sending me some bitchy email—big deal. What are they gonna do? I'm the one signing the checks.

It's a different life. When somebody doesn't like a deal, their lawyers sit down with my lawyers, they work it out at a few hundred bucks an hour, then they send everybody a bill. At the end of the day I go home to have dinner with my educated and beautiful wife. After that, most nights I hit the heavy bag. Then maybe I'll pour a drink, look out at the ocean, and just fucking laugh out loud. You figure the angles, then you follow your gut. I'm blessed, that's for sure.

When you wanna climb the ranks in kickboxing, you do what you say you're gonna do. When you're smuggling pot, you get it right the first time 'cos there's no second time. If it all goes to shit, "sorry" makes for a bruised and bloody answer. Living under that kind of pressure made me into the guy who, a few years later, could walk into a boardroom and come out with what I wanted. Those years were my version of going to college. It was a hell of a thing.

When I walked out of prison, my time on the other side of the law was over, and my escape was complete. I became a self-made three-time champ: in the ring, in the boardroom, and in the badass business of smuggling.

I can look back at the whole fucking thing with a smile. I walked away wealthy and I walked away clean. Forever.

And here I am.

EPILOGUE: JUST ME

Remember that scene at the end of *Goodfellas?* Mobster Henry Hill had spent a lifetime outside the law. The prize was he could get whatever he wanted, whenever he wanted it. When we were running marijuana, we had it all, too: money, access, power, influence. We could go wherever we wanted, whenever we wanted, and on those rare occasions we couldn't, we bargained, bought, or flat-out broke the rules to finish the job. Henry Hill figured the straight life would be the end of the good times. Not me. I figured out I could still live the high life, even higher than I did when I was smuggling. Plus I wouldn't have to keep looking over my shoulder.

Once I left that life, I never wanted to go back. When I walked out of prison, it was time for something better. Henry Hill just wasn't willing to work for it. I was, and I still am. As the '80s wound down, I knew that I was capable of anything I set my mind to, only now I'd walk in the front door instead of unloading a boat in the back. I'd turned away from a whole way of living, but one part remained: at heart, I would always be an entrepreneur. And I made it fucking work. I got the money, I got the prestige, I got the satisfaction of doing it right. And I didn't have to hide anything from anybody.

I had only a couple regrets. I wish I'd been able to do more for my mother when she was dying of cancer. All the money in the world wouldn't have saved her, but for a long time I believed it was my fault for not making enough money to somehow buy a miracle. It took me years to understand otherwise. My other regret is that my father saw me in prison. He took an eight-hour bus ride to spend a few hours with me, and that day broke his heart. The saving grace is that it was only a handful of years later that he saw me turn things around. I got to make him proud again. And I hope that somehow my mother knows what I've achieved and that she's proud, too.

Other than that? I don't regret one damn thing.

When I was in the tenth grade, my teacher wrote in my yearbook, "Least likely to succeed." Pretty nasty, but there's a lesson there: just because you have problems now doesn't mean you can't beat them tomorrow. The past is always past. The way forward starts with the now—with showing people what you can do today.

If anybody's waiting for me to say I'm sorry, keep waiting. I'm still standing, still fighting, and I always will be. You're either the champ or the chump, and that chump is looking up from the canvas. He's down there on his back.

And I've never been on my back.

ACKNOWLEDGMENTS

In my life I either know how to do something, learn how to do something, or find the smartest people I can to do it for me. A couple years ago I decided to write this book, but I didn't know squat about how to do it. Turns out my old friend Jordan Zimmerman was the key to the whole thing. He introduced me to Michael Long, who worked on Jordan's book (*Leading Fearlessly*—you should read it). Michael and I spent hours talking about my life. He converted all those conversations into the story you have in your hands—and, hopefully, something coming soon to a screen near you.

As for the folks from my days kickboxing and smuggling, I want to thank them, too, especially attorney Jon Sale, who remains my friend after all these years and who contributed wise counsel to this book. Not only as my counsel but I look at him as my big brother. As I wrote at the outset, there are several folks I want to acknowledge, but they would prefer to remain anonymous than to see their names anywhere near a memoir of the crazy shit we did four decades ago. I can't blame ya, guys. You know who you are. Thanks, one more time.

On the publishing side, thanks to the team at BenBella: Glenn Yeffeth, who encouraged us from the first read; Leah Wilson; Claire Schulz; Adrienne Lang; Sarah Avinger; Scott Calamar; James Fraleigh, who's a real hero when it comes to refining a manuscript into a great book; Rachel Phares; Isabelle Rubio; and everyone else there who worked hard for us. Thanks, too, to the team at Zimmerman Advertising. Jordan put them at our disposal. I couldn't have done this without that bunch of generous geniuses, and that's truly what they are.

The greatest thing about my life is my children: Teddy, Samantha, Jai-lin, Shaylee, and William. I'm blessed with a great family whom I love very much. Thanks to all of you.

Finally, thanks to my wife, Shien-Lin Pryor. You are my heart. When my brother passed, half my heart was gone. You gave me the love and strength to carry on. You are the kindest, most loving person in the world, and the light of my heart. I love you.

And to my brother: God love ya, Tony. See you again someday. Just so you know, the champ's still standing.

Author proceeds from the sale of this book go to the Pryor Family Foundation. There are too many kids out there who need help in a thousand ways, and there always will be. We're helping kids and their families who can't pay the rent. We're helping children who need more out of their educational childcare. We're even fighting human trafficking. I know what it is to be the child left behind in school, and that's why this matters to me. The foundation is changing lives. Here's a QR code that will take you to ThePryorFamilyFoundation.org. At the site you can learn more about our work, which you've supported by purchasing this book.

There's more to the story, much more. If you'd like to see videos from my fights and movies, plus more photos and memorabilia, visit TedPryor.com.

ABOUT THE AUTHOR

Former middleweight kickboxing champion of the world, **Ted Pryor** is the founder and retired CEO of one of the largest child education providers in the United States. He is also an entrepreneur, film producer, adventurer, and convicted marijuana smuggler. He lives in Florida, California, Hawaii, and Italy.